APEC

New Agenda in Its Third Decade

The **Institute of Southeast Asian Studies (ISEAS)** was established as an autonomous organization in 1968. It is a regional centre dedicated to the study of socio-political, security and economic trends and developments in Southeast Asia and its wider geostrategic and economic environment. The Institute's research programmes are the Regional Economic Studies (RES, including ASEAN and APEC), Regional Strategic and Political Studies (RSPS), and Regional Social and Cultural Studies (RSCS).

ISEAS Publishing, an established academic press, has issued more than 2,000 books and journals. It is the largest scholarly publisher of research about Southeast Asia from within the region. ISEAS Publishing works with many other academic and trade publishers and distributors to disseminate important research and analyses from and about Southeast Asia to the rest of the world.

APEC
New Agenda in Its Third Decade

Ippei Yamazawa

INSTITUTE OF SOUTHEAST ASIAN STUDIES
SINGAPORE

First published in Singapore in 2012 by
ISEAS Publishing
Institute of Southeast Asian Studies
30 Heng Mui Keng Terrace
Pasir Panjang
Singapore 119614

E-mail: publish@iseas.edu.sg
Website: <http://bookshop.iseas.edu.sg>

ISEAS Library Cataloguing-in-Publication Data

Yamazawa, Ippei, 1937–
APEC : new agenda in its third decade.
1. Asia Pacific Economic Cooperation (Organization).
I. Title.
HF1583 Y211 2012

ISBN 978-981-4311-63-2 (soft cover)
ISBN 978-981-4311-64-9 (E-book PDF)

Typeset by Superskill Graphics Pte Ltd
Printed in Singapore by Mainland Press Pte Ltd

Contents

Figures and Tables

Figures

Tables

Preface

The Asia-Pacific Economic Cooperation's (APEC) momentum heightened in 1993–96. In 1993 in Seattle, the United States hosted the first APEC Economic Leaders' Meeting. In 1994 in Bogor, Indonesia, the leaders issued the ambitious statement of "the industrialized economies achieving the goal of free and open trade and investment no later than the year 2010 and developing economies no later than the year 2020". The Osaka Action Agenda was adopted in 1995 and the Manila Framework was adopted in 1996. However, ASEAN (Association of Southeast Asian Nations) and other Asian members were hit severely by the East Asian currency crisis in 1997–98, while APEC's liberalization agenda turned out to be much less than had been expected. Both leaders' meetings and ministerial meetings have continued to be held in one of the APEC member economies in autumn every year, but the media only report the leaders' statements. APEC has developed a pragmatic agenda for regional economic cooperation focusing on business facilitation and has achieved steady expansion of trade and investment in the region through its second decade.

Globalization has continued in terms of money, business, and people. While trying to overcome the current world financial crisis, all economies need to cooperate on such new global issues as global warming, pandemics, poverty, and human security. The G-20 Summit emerged in 2008 as a new global consultation forum for global governance, in addition to the United Nations, International Monetary Fund, World Bank, World Trade Organization, and World Health Organization, while APEC and other regional cooperation bodies are expected to supplement them.

APEC was hosted by Singapore in 2009, Japan in 2010, and will be hosted by the United States in 2011. It expects capable hosts to successfully tackle the new challenges in the beginning of its third decade. Japan took the lead in the assessment of the mid-term achievement of the Bogor

Goals in 2010 and paved the way towards the Free Trade Area of the Asia Pacific Region (FTAAP). With strengthened U.S. engagement, negotiations among nine APEC members for the Trans-Pacific Partnership (TPP) began in 2010. Following Singapore's lead in addressing the desirable attributes for growth in the region, Yokohama APEC announced the APEC Growth Strategy as the post-Bogor agenda.

However, these efforts are currently not well known to media and the general public in the region. Those who remember the heightened APEC momentum in the 1990s will ask, "So what happened to the Bogor Goals?" This book answers this question and details the current achievements of APEC in tackling these new challenges.

The book is organized as follows: Chapter 1 presents an overview of APEC's current agenda. At the onset of the current global financial crisis in the autumn of 2008, the APEC Lima Meeting responded in a timely manner to the G-20 Summit's call with a package of macroeconomic policy and financial stability measures. The APEC Singapore Meeting picked up a variety of issues requiring global responses, such as "inclusive growth" to address issues of increasing income disparity, poverty under globalization, and environmental protection. APEC Yokohama announced the mid-term assessment of APEC's progress towards the Bogor Goals and the post-Bogor agenda.

Chapters 2 to 5 examine the main activities of APEC, trade and investment liberalization and facilitation. Chapter 2 reviews its activities of the past twenty years, focusing on its unique modality of liberalization. Chapter 3 analyses the organizational details of APEC in comparison with the European Union. It also explains the private sector's participation in APEC. Chapter 4 presents the author's quantitative assessment of APEC's progress towards the Bogor Goals, together with APEC's group assessment of the thirteen economies in 2010. Chapter 5 explains current pragmatic approaches, such as various activities in response to prevalent free trade agreements, economic and technical cooperation, and domestic reform for behind-the-border measures.

Chapter 6 discusses the post-Bogor agenda in pursuance of Chapter 1. How can we further develop APEC's liberalization through the Trans-Pacific Partnership (TPP) and FTAAP?

Chapter 7 discusses interaction between APEC and the East Asian Community (EAC). The paradigm of East Asian regional cooperation shifted towards the EAC since the East Asian currency crisis in 1997–98.

But building the EAC will take time, due to insufficient capability of its leading members, immature cooperation among another group, and the unresolved difficulty of handling external partners. This chapter will argue how to utilize APEC and the TPP in parallel with the EAC towards Asia-Pacific integration.

APEC's advantage is its vast membership across the Pacific, including major industrialized and developing economies. And APEC has twenty years of experience in technical assistance in facilitation and eco-technology. Although it needs to strengthen aspects of liberalization through a pathfinder approach, its main modality of non-binding principles and open regionalism will continue to tackle the current and new cooperation agendas.

Forty years have passed since the author started to study Pacific economic cooperation following his mentor, the late Professor Kiyoshi Kojima. He has benefitted from recurrent discussion and communication with his colleagues in the Pacific Trade and Development Conference, Pacific Economic Cooperation Conference, APEC Eminent Persons Group, and APEC Study Center. He sincerely wishes more from the younger generation will join and further promote the study. This book will be his last contribution to this study, which he would like to devote to all of them.

The first draft of this book in Japanese was published in August 2010 by JETRO in the preparation for APEC 2010 Yokohama. This English book was drafted based on its Japanese edition but substantially rewritten and enlarged in order to update and include the heightened discussion of Trans-Pacific Partnership negotiation for the past several months so as to be published in time for APEC 2011 Honolulu.

The author would like to express his sincere thanks to the Institute of Southeast Asian Studies for this publication and its editor Stephen Logan for careful and extensive editing.

Ippei Yamazawa
May 2011

Abbreviations

3T	Telecommunication, Transportation, and Tourism
ABAC	APEC Business Advisory Council
ABTC	APEC Business Travel Card
ABTH	*APEC Business Travel Handbook*
ADB	Asian Development Bank
AFAS	ASEAN Framework Agreement on Services
AFTA	ASEAN Free Trade Area
APEC	Asia-Pacific Economic Cooperation
APIAN	APEC International Assessment Network
ASCC	APEC Study Center Consortium
ASEAN	Association of Southeast Asian Nations
ATIGA	ASEAN Trade in Goods Agreement
C-J-ROK	China-Japan-Republic of Korea
CAP	Collective Action Plan
CEP	comprehensive economic partnership
CEPEA	Comprehensive Economic Partnership for East Asia
CER	Closer Economic Relationship
CGE	computable general equilibrium
CMI	Chiang Mai Initiative
COP	Conference of the Parties
CTI	Committee for Trade and Investment
CUL	concerted unilateral liberalization
DDA	Doha Development Agenda
DRR	Disaster Risk Reduction
EAC	East Asian community
EAEC	East Asian Economic Caucus
EAFTA	East Asia Free Trade Area
EAS	East Asia Summit
EAVG	East Asian Vision Group

ECFA	Economic Cooperation Framework Agreement
EDIFACT	Electronic Data Interchange for Administration, Commerce and Transport
EODB	Ease of Doing Business
EPA	Economic Partnership Agreement
EPG	Eminent Persons Group
ESC	Ecotech Subcommittee
ESTA	Electronic System for Travel Authorization
EVSL	Early Voluntary Sector Liberalization
FDI	foreign direct investment
FTA	free trade agreement/free trade area
FTAA	Free Trade Area of the Americas
FTAAP	Free Trade Area of the Asia-Pacific
GATS	General Agreement in Trade in Services
GATT	General Agreement on Tariffs and Trade
GDP	gross domestic product
GPA	Government Procurement Agreement
HSC	Harmonized Standard Classification
IAEG	International Atomic Energy Commission
IAP	Individual Action Plan
IEC	International Electrotechnical Commission
IFAP	Investment Facilitation Action Plan
IMF	International Monetary Fund
IPR	intellectual property rights
ISO	International Organization for Standardization
JACEP	Japan-ASEAN Comprehensive Economic Partnership
KIEP	Korean Institute of International Economic Policy
LAISR	Leaders' Agenda to Implement Structural Reform
LPI	Logistics Performance Index
MAPA	Manila Action Plan for APEC
METI	Ministry of Economy, Trade, and Industry, Japan
MFN	most favoured nation
MM	Ministerial Meeting
MRA	Mutual Recognition Agreement
MRT	Ministers Responsible for Trade
MTST	Mid-Term Stock-Take
NAFTA	North American Free Trade Area

NBIP	non-binding investment principles
NTM	non-tariff measures
OAA	Osaka Action Agenda
ODA	official development assistance
OECD	Organization for Economic Cooperation and Development
PAFTAD	Pacific Trade and Development Conference
PASC	Pacific Association for Standards and Conformance
PBEC	Pacific Basin Economic Council
PBF	Pacific Business Forum
PECC	Pacific Economic Cooperation Council
PFP	Partners for Progress
PMC	Post Ministerial Conference
PNG	Papua New Guinea
ROO	Rules of Origin
RTA	Regional Trade Agreement
S&C	standards and conformance
SAA	Stabilisation and Association Agreement
SCCP	Subcommittee on Custom Procedures
SCSC	Subcommittee for Standards and Conformance
SME	small and medium enterprises
SOM	Senior Officials' Meeting
STAR	Secure Trade in APEC Regions
TAC	Treaty of Amity and Cooperation
TFAP	Trade Facilitation Action Plan
TFEP	Task Force on Emergency Preparedness
TILF	trade and investment liberalization and facilitation
TPP	Trans-Pacific Strategic Partnership
TPRM	Trade Policy Review Mechanism
TPSEP	Trans-Pacific Strategic Economic Partnership
TRIM	trade related investment measures
TRIPS	Trade-Related Aspects of Intellectual Property Rights
UR	Uruguay Round
URA	Uruguay Round Agreement
USTR	Office of the United States Trade Representative
VAP	Voluntary Arrangement for the Pacific
WCO	World Customs Organization
WTO	World Trade Organization

1

Current State of APEC and the Challenges Ahead

Main Features of the APEC Economies

APEC, or the Asia-Pacific Economic Cooperation Forum is the largest intergovernmental framework for economic cooperation in the Asia-Pacific region. Currently twenty-one economies participate in it: Australia, Brunei, Canada, Chile, China, Hong Kong, Indonesia, Japan, South Korea (Republic of Korea), Malaysia, Mexico, New Zealand, Papua New Guinea (PNG), Peru, the Philippines, Russia, Singapore, Chinese Taipei (the designated name used by Taiwan to participate in APEC), Thailand, the United States, and Vietnam.[1] It covers a vast area surrounding the Pacific Ocean as is shown in Figure 1.1.

The following three key words characterize APEC: **diversity**, **high growth**, and **non-institutionalization**. The vast variety of participating economies is the most distinct characteristics of this group. Table 1.1 gives the main indicators of the twenty-one APEC economies. The 2007 figures are taken in order to avoid its structure being distorted by the world financial crisis caused by the Lehman shock in autumn 2008.

APEC economies differ greatly in area and resource endowment. Russia has the biggest area of 17 million square kilometres (sq. km), followed by Canada, the United States, and China each with more than

FIGURE 1.1
21 Economies Participating in APEC

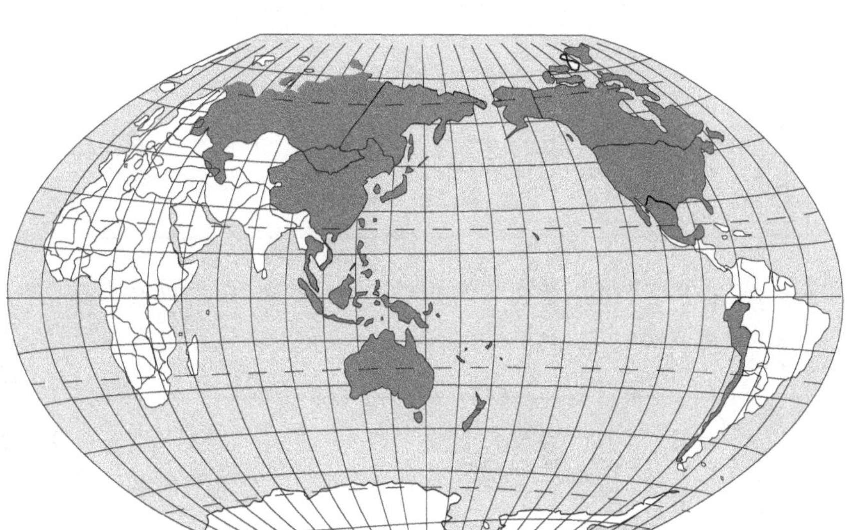

9 million sq. km, and Australia with 7.7 million sq. km. Of course, a large part of Russia and Canada are frozen desert in the Arctic zone, and Australia has a big dessert, but their possible endowment with large economic resources cannot be denied. At the other extreme, APEC has tiny city economies such as Singapore and Hong Kong.

In terms of population, China is the biggest with 1.3 billion people, making 49 per cent of the total population of APEC, followed by the United States and Indonesia each with less than a quarter of China's population, and Russia and Japan with one tenth of China's population. Brunei is the smallest with 380,000, followed by Singapore and New Zealand with 4 million each. In terms of GDP, the United States is the biggest with US$13.7 trillion, followed by Japan with US$4.4 trillion, and the two combined economies accounted for 61 per cent of APEC's total GDP.

TABLE 1.1
Economic Indicators of APEC Economies, 2007

	Population (million)	Area (1,000 km)	GDP (US$ billion)	Per capita (US$)	Growth rate (annual, real %) 1995–2001	2001–07
Japan	127.4	378	4,380.38	34,383	0.84	1.78
China	1,306.13	9,561	3,460.29	2,649	8.22	10.16
South Korea	47.96	99	1,294.38	26,989	4.21	4.68
Hong Kong	6.95	1	207.17	29,809	2.2	5.44
Chinese Taipei	22.92	36	393.13	17,152	4.15	5.43
Brunei	0.38	6	12.28	32,316	1.54	2.07
Indonesia	224.67	1,905	432.92	1,927	1.19	5.16
Malaysia	26.56	330	186.72	7,030	3.98	5.74
The Philippines	88.72	300	144.06	1,624	3.5	5.39
Singapore	4.48	1	166.95	37,266	4.77	6.51
Thailand	66.98	513	246.05	3,673	0.72	5.44
Vietnam	86.11	331	71.01	825	6.71	7.59
Australia	20.85	7,713	947.36	45,437	3.8	3.27
New Zealand	4.19	271	130.43	31,129	2.77	3.41
PNG	6.42	463	6.2	966	0.61	3.16
Canada	32.95	9,971	1,429.71	43,390	3.68	2.73
Chile	16.64	757	163.92	9,851	3.94	4.41
Mexico	107.49	1,964	1,019.35	9,483	4.41	2.84
Peru	28.51	1,280	107.33	3,765	2.08	6.04
USA	308.67	9,364	13,741.60	44,519	3.49	2.55
Russia	141.94	16,889	1,294.38	9,119	2.14	6.65
APEC total	2,676.92		29,835.62			

Note: Real growth rates are calculated from GDP by type of expenditure at constant (1990) prices in U.S. dollars.
Sources: United Nations Statstical Division, National Accounts Estimates of Main Aggregates, online, supplemented by Taiwan's statistics online <www.stat.gov.tw>.

There is a vast difference in per capita income, which is calculated by dividing GDP by population size. Australia, the United States and Canada are the highest over $40,000, followed by Singapore, Japan, Brunei, and New Zealand each with over $30,000, Hong Kong and South Korea with $27,000–29,000, Chinese Taipei with $17,000, Chile, Mexico, and Russia with $9,000, Malaysia with $7,000, and Thailand with $3,700. China has caught up to hit $2,600, while Indonesia and the Philippines stay at less than $2,000, and PNG and Vietnam at less than $1,000. Incidenatlly, the APEC average per capita income is $11,149. This difference in per capita income and the resulting difference in living standards reflect their different stages of development.

The two columns of Table 1.1 in the right give real growth rates for the past twelve years. Three benchmark years of 1995, 2001, and 2007 are selected in order to avoid the disturbances of the Asian currency crisis in 1997–98, and the world financial crisis in 2008–09. However, ASEAN (Association of Southeast Asian Nations) members had not recovered fully from the currency crisis in 2001, so their growth rates in the first period were as low as 1–2 per cent. But in the following six years, Asian economies except for Japan, grew at over 5 per cent. China, in particular, grew at 10 per cent and Vietnam at 7 per cent, followed by Russia, Chile, Peru, and Mexico growing at between 3 and 4 per cent. On the other hand, the industrialized economies of the United States, Australia, Canada, and New Zealand grew at 2–3 per cent, and Japan registered the lowest growth of all throughout the two periods. Incidentally the European Union grew at 2.65 per cent and 1.95 per cent respectively. The Asian economies were not affected very much by the world financial crisis in 2008–09, and China and other developing economies in East Asia pulled up the growth rate of the APEC region.

Diversity has both its merits and demerits. On the merit side, diversity in resource endowment and different living standards have brought a complementality and encouraged trade and investment. The Asian developing economies achieved high growth, demonstrating the so-called "East Asian Miracle" for the ten years before the Asian currency crisis. Industrialized economies maintained a higher growth through the export of primary products and technology-intensive and high value-added products to these developing economies. Interdependence among the APEC economies has deepened while still promoting their region's high growth. The high growth potential of East Asian developing economies had provided the biggest incentive for forming APEC, which aims at realizing this high growth potential.

On the other hand, the downside of diversity is that their differences tend to make mutual understanding between participants difficult and consensus building and collective actions take time. As a matter of fact, APEC could not have started with an institutional structure, that is, *non-institutionalization* was the only option. However, some experts argue that APEC, with its flexible approach, could have fostered regional integration among diverse participants.

Nevertheless, APEC has tended to be misunderstood or underestimated because of its non-institutionalization. It is self-evident that, with its participants and current progress that will be analysed later, APEC, together with the European Union, is expected to lift the world economy up from the crisis. The combined GDP for APEC's twenty-one economies amounted to US$30 trillion in 2007, with East Asia contributing 37 per cent, or US$11 trillion. On the other hand, the economies of North America, Chile, and Peru combined and the European Union each had a GDP of US$16 trillion, followed by East Asia with two-thirds of this. APEC should not be underestimated simply because it is not institutionalized. These three key words are interrelated.

APEC's Responses to the Global Financial Crisis

In November 2008, APEC responded in a timely manner to the expanding global economic crisis. In the G-20 Leaders' Summit held on 15 November in Washington D.C., the leaders decided to take urgent measures to stabilize financial markets and to carry out coordinated macroeconomic policies to restore growth and stability. The following week, at the APEC Leaders' Meeting which was held in Lima, Peru, the Lima APEC Leaders' Statement on the Global Economy (APEC/LM 2008) was issued. In the statement, APEC leaders strongly supported the Washington Declaration of the G-20 leaders and their action plan. APEC leaders were committed to take the broad policy responses needed to overcome the current crisis within eighteen months, and reiterated their firm belief that free market principles and open trade and investment regimes should continue to be the measures to drive growth, employment, and fight poverty.

The G-20 Summit is expected to be the new framework underlying the management of the global economy. An expanded version of the G-8, it is a collaborative framework on a global scale, involving major emerging economies such as China, India, and Brazil, plus mid-sized economies such as Australia and South Korea. The G-20 needs to be supported by APEC and other major regional groups in order to ensure that the goals of the G-20 commitment are achieved. Nine APEC economies participated in the G-20, thus providing a driving force for the framework. APEC has, however, not only been a framework for consensus building over policy coordination among participating economies, but has also been providing assistance to developing economies by way of technology transfer and capacity building.

In addition, there is an advantage of overlapping. The G-20 will be tasked in future to address issues such as environmental protection, disaster management, infectious disease prevention, antiterrorism, poverty eradication, and so on. These issues have already been addressed in the APEC framework. Nevertheless, APEC is expected to contribute by cooperating closely with the G-20 to meet these challenges.

The G-20 Summit has been held semi-annually; once in Seoul, South Korea in the week preceding the Yokohama APEC in October 2010. Leaders have been discussing how to tackle the global uncertainty caused by the Lehman shock and the euro crisis. They acknowledged the dynamic growth of emerging economies, but addressed the need for closer policy cooperation in correcting imbalances of saving-investment and current accounts between the United States and Asia. The APEC Growth Strategy adopted by APEC Leaders in Yokohama in 2010 addressed "balanced growth" as the priority policy agenda (APEC/LM 2010c).

APEC's Momentum Returning

APEC economies take turns to host the forum every year. Almost all member economies have hosted APEC once, and Thailand, Australia, and Singapore have hosted it twice. In 2010 Japan hosts APEC and in 2011 the United States will do so, both for the second time. While APEC faces big challenges to be tackled together amidst the global crisis, the hosting of APEC for three successive years 2009–11 by capable economies is welcome and encouraging.

APEC's momentum is returning, as evidenced by several events and developments. President Obama visited Japan, China, and South Korea on his way to and from the APEC Leaders' Meeting in 2009, stressing clearly U.S. interest in Asia in his address in Tokyo. He also joined the first ASEAN-U.S. Summit in Singapore. Prime Minister Hatoyama renewed Japan's initiative for the East Asian Community in his address in Singapore, which will incorporate the U.S. interest in Asia. APEC leaders confirmed their intention to work together towards strong, sustainable, and balanced economic growth, in close cooperation with the G-20 Summit. APEC finance ministers also met for the first time at the time of the Leaders' Meeting to discuss details of their cooperation.

In Tokyo, President Obama stated the United States' commitment as a Pacific nation to Asia, both in terms of its security and prosperity, in a shift to a new U.S.-Asia relationship in the twenty-first century (Obama 2009). While "strengthening old alliances" with Japan, South Korea, Australia, Thailand, and the Philippines, the United States also "perceives the emergence of China", and seeks to "cultivate spheres of cooperation". The United States continues to promote regional commerce and prosperity within APEC and looks forward to engaging with EAS (East Asia Summit) and TPP countries. With his summit dialogue with ASEAN leaders, he welcomed the successful cooperation with ASEAN for the past thirty-two years and stated that the United States is committed to supporting the ASEAN Community plans, while ASEAN leaders welcomed the U.S. accession to the Treaty of Amity and Cooperation (TAC). The United States perceived ASEAN's growing capacity and role in global issues and supported regional efforts initiated by ASEAN and ASEAN-led fora.

Throughout 2010, APEC SOM (Senior Officials' Meeting) conducted a detailed survey and analysis of the mid-term assessment of the Bogor Goals by thirteen economies (five industrialized and eight volunteered). The leaders jointly declared that they had made good progress and that APEC as a whole achieved the most dynamic growth and played the driving role for the global economy. Nevertheless, they noted that several sensitive sectors still remain to be liberalized and deregulated and they committed to continuing the TILF (trade and investment liberalization and facilitation) process towards the final target of 2020 (APEC/LM 2010b).

Yokohama APEC also addressed the "APEC Growth Strategy", which emphasizes the five attributes of desirable growth for the Asia Pacific region: balanced, inclusive, sustainable, innovative, and secure. They proposed an action plan to implement them and instructed SOM to make a progress report by 2015. This will be another big goal for APEC as part of the post-Bogor agenda. The implementation of this has been handed to the United States, APEC host for 2011.

Note

1. Incidentally, they are termed "economies", rather than "countries/regions", and "participants" but not "members" in APEC.

2

Trade and Investment Liberalization and Facilitation

Origin of Regional Cooperation in the Asia Pacific

The origin of economic cooperation in the Asia Pacific dates back to 1967–68. In five countries surrounding the Pacific a business group formed a conference series of the Pacific Basin Economic Council (PBEC) in 1967 and an economist group formed another conference series of the Pacific Trade and Development Conference (PAFTAD). They were stimulated by the successful development in Europe and aimed to study and discuss economic cooperation and integration in the Pacific. The first PFTD conference was organized by its proponent Professor Kiyoshi Kojima in Tokyo, and in its second conference in Honolulu, scholars from South Korea, Taiwan, and other Southeast Asian countries participated.[1] Both conference series were hosted by different countries in turn and discussed a variety of cooperation issues in the Pacific, but neither of them had any participation from governments.

In 1978 Japanese Prime Minister Masayaoshi Ohira proposed the "Pacific Basin Community" idea in his inaugural speech, which paved the way for individual governments to participate in the discussion. Interest in the cooperation of Pacific nations spread from businessmen and economists to diplomats, international relations scholars, and journalists.

In Japan a study group was formed to give substance to the Ohira proposal and it published a report a year later (Pacific Basin Community Study Group Report 1979). Prime Minister Ohira and his Foreign Minister Saburo Ohkita visited Australia and New Zealand, bringing with them the report. Australian Prime Minister Malcom Fraser and his advisor Sir John Crawford (vice-chancellor of the Australian National University) agreed with Ohira and Ohkita on the promotion of the cooperation of Pacific nations so that a Canberra Seminar on the Pacific Basin Community was organized in 1980. Both Ohkita and Crawford were co-founders of PAFTAD together with Kojima and this personal link helped to start the Pacific nations cooperation, which commenced with a series of Pacific Economic Cooperation Conference (PECC).

At the beginning the PECC attracted participation from eleven countries and regions: Japan, Australia, New Zealand, the United States, Canada, as well as South Korea and five ASEAN countries. China and Taiwan participated in 1986. Formed by three parties of business, academic, and government officials and hosted by one of the participating countries every one and a half years, it studied and discussed a variety of cooperation issues in the Pacific. It announced a few important statements on the desired direction of cooperation, but was without any enforcement power. It followed and supported market-driven integration in the region and focused on voluntary liberalization and technical cooperation. PBEC members represented the business group, while PAFTAD members represented academics, and the two were the major stakeholders of PECC.

APEC in its First Decade

In 1989, APEC started taking shape as a series of meetings by the foreign and trade ministers of twelve member nations to discuss economic cooperation matters in the Asia-Pacific region. Over the past twenty years, it has witnessed ebbs and flows in its momentum of cooperation.

Trade and investment liberalization and facilitation (TILF) has become one of APEC's major tasks since the first Economic Leaders' Meeting in Seattle in 1993, when leaders jointly declared that they would "achieve free and open trade in Asia and Pacific". At the second Leaders' Meeting in Bogor, Indonesia, President Soeharto delivered the ambitious Bogor Declaration, "to complete the achievement of our goal of free and open trade and investment in the Asia-Pacific no later than the year 2020,

...with the industrialized economies achieving the goal of free and open trade and investment no later than the year 2010 and developing economies no later than the year 2020" (APEC Leaders' Declaration 1994). In 1995, the Osaka APEC adopted the Osaka Action Agenda (OAA), which provided concrete measures that could be taken to achieve the Bogor Goals.

The Committee for Trade and Investment (CTI) provided a common format in 1996 for Individual Action Plans (IAPs), in which individual governments of participating economies announced their own programmes to be implemented in accordance with the OAA. CTI also produced a Collective Action Plan (CAP) regarding measures to be implemented collectively, such as harmonized legislatures and systems. Thus IAPs included individual members' participation in CAP as well. The Manila APEC in November 1996 approved IAPs submitted by all member governments (Manila Action Plan for APEC, or MAPA) and their implementation started in 1997.

The annual APEC gathering of prime ministers and presidents of major economies with their bold declarations attracted media attention and expectations of APEC heightened. The number of participating economies increased to twenty-one in 1998 and included all major economies surrounding the Pacific Ocean.

However, APEC encountered a big setback during the Asian financial crisis when several ASEAN (Association of Southeast Asian Nations) members and South Korea were severely hit, with their currencies depreciating substantially, and some even suffering from negative growth. The EVSL (Early Voluntary Sector Liberalization) plan, a breakthrough attempt at liberalization in the "easy sectors", also failed.[2] As such, the IAPs implemented since 1997 brought about much less liberalization than had been expected. Although it included the liberalization committed in the Uruguay Round Agreement (URA), its unilateral liberalization beyond the URA to other APEC members and non-members alike has been limited in terms of both coverage and depth. The URA liberalization was implemented on schedule as committed, but further liberalization in sensitive sectors tended to be suspended. The Doha Development Agenda (DDA) negotiations which started in 2002 has also been protracted in recent years.

On the other hand, APEC itself has shifted to a more realistic line of action for the past decade. Its focus has shifted from liberalization to trade facilitation, capacity building, and structural reforms. The business environment has also changed in the Asia Pacific amidst accelerated globalization and the prevailing regionalism of bilateral and subregional preferential trading arrangements. The Busan Roadmap announced in 2005 includes these realistic measures.

Bogor Goals as APEC's Engine for TILF

APEC has pursued its liberalization and facilitation measures towards achieving the Bogor Goal within the IAP/CAP framework. Its concrete design, the OAA, had comprehensive coverage of fourteen areas of trade and investment liberalization and facilitation (see Table 2.1), and described measures to be implemented for each area. Facilitation measures aim to reduce the cost of doing business by enhancing the transparency and certainty of rules, legislation, and standards, and harmonizing them among participating economies, which are equally important to liberalization in order to enhance trade and investment in the region.

The IAP formula reflected APEC's unique modality of implementing liberalization and facilitation, that of "concerted unilateral liberalization" (CUL). Under this scheme individual economies unilaterally announced their own liberalization and facilitation programmes and implemented them in accordance with their domestic rules. However, individual economies closely watched one another's liberalization programme and implementation, and were obliged to submit liberalization programmes as broad ranging as their neighbours and were encouraged to implement these in line with their commitments. SOM has been conducting a peer review process of individual IAPs at its special sessions since 2002. APEC relies on peer pressure to urge all economies to join in the liberalization efforts.

The governments of individual economies have continued to revise their IAPs every year. The reporting has been made more elaborate, and transparency has improved in response to a common format. The number of liberalization measures increased as their Uruguay Round (UR) commitments were implemented. Voluntary liberalization was also added, either in the form of the accelerated implementation of the URA, or the reduction of applied tariffs from their UR rates in several economies. The CAP helped individual economies to introduce common practices such as the Summary Tables of Tariffs and NTMs (non-tariff measures). CAP was especially effective in introducing new legislation of facilitation, consistent with the APEC system prescribed in the OAA. By and large, the IAP process encouraged the governments of individual economies to implement

TABLE 2.1
Chronology of APEC Development

Late 1960s:	Proposals for Pacific Economic Cooperation; PBEC (1967) and (1968).
1978:	Proposal for Pacific Economic Community by Japanese Prime Minister Ohira. Report of PEC Study Group (1979).
1980:	The first Pacific Economic Cooperation Council (PECC) Meeting (Canberra).
1989:	Asia Pacific Economic Cooperation (APEC) Ministerial Meeting started Canberra, Australia) with 12 members (Australia, Canada, Japan, New Zealand, the United States, Republic of Korea, and 6 ASEAN members).
1990:	APECII (Singapore).
1991:	APECIII (Seoul, South Korea); China, Hong Kong, and Chinese Taipei joined. Seoul Declaration issued.
1992:	APECIV (Bangkok, Thailand); Eminent Persons Group established.
1993:	APECV (Seattle, United States); Informal Economic Leaders Meeting; Mexico joined.
1994:	APECVI (Jakarta/Bogor); Bogor Declaration, PNG and Chile joined.
1995:	APECVII (Osaka, Japan); Osaka Action Agenda adopted with Initital Actions announced.
1996:	APECVIII (Subic, the Philippines); Manila Action Plan for APEC (MAPA) announced and implemented by individual members.
1997:	APECIX (Vancouver, Canada).
1998:	APECX (Kuala Lumpur, Malaysia) EVSL failed. Peru, Russia, and Vietnam joined.
1999:	APECXI (Auckland, New Zealand) APEC Principle for promoting Competition Policy and Deregulation adopted.
2000:	APECXII (Brunei).
2001:	APECXIII (Shanghai, China) TFAP adopted.
2002:	APECXIV (Mexico).
2003:	APECXV (Thailand).
2004:	APECXVI (Santiago, Chile).
2005:	APECXVII (Busan, South Korea); MTST conducted and Busan Road Map towards achieving the Bogor Goals adopted.
2006:	APECXVIII (Hanoi, Vietnam) Hanoi Action Plan and LAISR announced.
2007:	APECXIX (Sydney, Australia) SREI report adopted.
2008:	APECXX (Lima, Peru) RTAs/FTAs model measures finalized.
2009:	APECXXI (Singapore) Inclusive growth proposed.
2010:	APECXXII (Yokohama, Japan).
2011:	APECXXIII (Honolulu, United States).
2012:	APECXXIV (Vladivostok, Russia).

liberalization and facilitation measures for achieving the Bogor Goals. One shortcoming of such implementation was the "positive list formula", in which the IAP reported only the impediments to be liberalized, but not those still remaining. Thus the IAPs increased the volume, but did not provide a comprehensive list of existing impediments.[3]

Constrained Liberalization under Voluntariness

In PECC and APEC, trade liberalization is implemented voluntarily, unbound by any treaty, and applied on an MFN (most favoured nation) basis to both members and non-members alike. This voluntary, non-binding principle and open regionalism constitute a unique modality of liberalization in APEC. This is perfectly consistent with GATT/WTO (General Agreement on Tariffs and Trade/World Trade Organization) rules. APEC's strategy for liberalization aims to promote this modality and the multilateral trade negotiation under GATT/WTO in parallel. As a matter of fact, PECC supported strongly the launch of the Uruguay Round of negotiations in 1986. APEC pushed its conclusions in 1994, urged the launch of the new millennium round in the late 1990s, and contributed to the successful conclusion of the DDA for the past few years. In 2008 APEC echoed the statement by the G-20 Summit at the break of the global financial crisis so that protection measures should be suspended.

This is an ideal modality that fits well with the economic teaching that importers gain from liberalization. It has not only been accepted by Asian members, but has also had some success. While Asian economies set their GATT/WTO-bound tariffs relatively high, they lowered applied tariffs on actual imports.[4] However, when the Bogor Declaration was announced and its action agenda was discussed, conflicting ideas emerged. In the Eminent Persons Group, its American chairman Fred Bergsten argued that the Bogor Goals could not be achieved by non-binding, voluntary liberalization, and insisted on reciprocal tariff reductions such as in FTA (free trade agreement) negotiations. Other group members, including myself, insisted that the FTA was not yet accepted by Asian members, and that voluntary liberalization would be effective. As a result both formula were listed in the EPG Report III (1995).

"Open regionalism" became a good byword for APEC, conveying its open image, but it contains a contradiction in the sense that regionalism itself favours members, but discriminates against non-members. If renamed "open regional cooperation", APEC can be interpreted as conducting regional cooperation consistent with the multilateral rules of GATT/WTO. Since the FTA is allowed by GATT/WTO, the FTA method can be claimed to be consistent with open regionalism.

At first Japanese senior officials in charge of drafting the Osaka Action Agenda pursued the FTA approach to achieve the Bogor Goals, but they met with strong resistance from the agricultural sector at home, and a rejection of liberalization by many Asian economies, so they changed to the former approach of concerted unilateral liberalization. The United States and Australia, although insisting on binding liberalization at first, finally conceded to the Asian rejection.[5]

However, as we will see in Chapter 4, this formula could not achieve liberalization in sensitive sectors, such as agriculture in Japan and South Korea, textiles and clothing in the United States and Canada, and auto and steel in advanced developing economies in Asia. High tariffs still remain in these sensitive sectors and their reduction requires reciprocal reductions through WTO negotiations. The DDA itself has stumbled in the past few years, and bilateral and plurilateral FTAs have mushroomed instead. Sensitive sectors are also liberalized fully or partially in the latter negotiations, but they are applied not on an MFN basis, but only within FTAs.

The Free Trade Area of the Asia-Pacific (FTAAP) was proposed by ABAC's (APEC Business Advisory Council) American members in 2006. However, since Americans only had the FTA formula when they proposed liberalization to APEC in 1993, they simply resumed their original liberalization proposal. The FTAAP is now discussed as a post-Bogor agenda for APEC. Although I had insisted on concerted unilateral liberalization fifteen years ago, I support it now as a necessary step with some binding element towards furthering APEC's liberalization. The late Dr Hadi Soesastro, director of Indonesia's CSIS and theoretical leader of ASEAN economies, insisted that binding liberalization under FTAAP would not be accepted by ASEAN members. He used to say that APEC would have to move from v-APEC (voluntary) to b-APEC (binding) someday,[6] but insisted that ASEAN was not ready yet for the move.[7] When you consider that ASEAN plans to complete ASEAN Economic Community by 2015, was he not too cautious?

Promotion of TILF through the Peer Review Process

In 2002–04 APEC's senior officials meeting (SOM) conducted the second round of the peer review process of IAPs so as to strengthen their efforts towards achieving the Bogor Goals. A team was formed for each economy's IAP, comprising a senior official, one or two expert consultants, and an APEC Secretariat staff member. Based on comments submitted by other economies, the team interviewed government officials of the economy under review and drafted a peer review report. The report was then submitted to a special session of the SOM, chaired by the team's senior official, discussed in an open forum, and amended where necessary, thus encouraging the economy under review to improve its IAP implementation closer towards achieving the Bogor Goals.

Although individual teams followed a common format set by SOM for the peer-review report, and reviewed each economy's implementation by areas, the assessment stance differed between review teams. Many followed the WTO's Trade Policy Review Mechanism (TPRM) closely. The TPRM indicates departures of an economy's trade and investment policy from WTO rules, and urges an economy to close such gaps. Some reviewers have followed the TPRM closely but they have tended to be more lenient towards developing economies. APEC's IAP peer reviews should, however, differ from the TPRM. APEC's IAPs focus on an economy's liberalization and facilitation efforts, reflecting its unique domestic conditions, and do not request quick harmonization. Both the Bogor Goals and the OAA contain ambiguity and flexibility, some deliberate and some unintended. Hence, it does not fit into APEC's modality to redefine rules strictly and to decide which economy passes and which fails. Rather it should encourage as many economies as possible to continue in their efforts to attain the Bogor Goals. This seems to be the fundamental objective of the IAP Peer Review.[8] In the meantime, SOM conducted the second round of peer review in 2007–09.

In 2005 the host country, South Korea, conducted mid-term stocktaking of the IAPs in order to invigorate individual economies' efforts in achieving the Bogor Goals. Individual economies were asked to submit an assessment of their achievements by then. The South Korean Government's think tank, the Korean Institute of Economic Policy (KIEP), formed an international expert team to examine the issue. Peer review reports and individual economies' own assessment reports were analysed and the

KIEP team presented a detailed comparison of each individual economy's achievement on each of the thirteen areas of the OAA (APEC 2005*b*) and a summary of all APEC members' progress made towards achieving the Bogor Goals (APEC 2005*b*). SOM produced a mid-term stocktaking report and introduced a new action plan: the Busan Road Map (APEC 2005*a*). The report was submitted to the Ministerial Meeting and the leaders adopted the Busan Road Map.

Trade and Investment Expansion in the APEC Economies

We have already seen at the beginning of Chapter 1 that the APEC region has achieved high growth, led by China and other developing East Asian nations, since the end of the 1990s. Appendix Tables 1 and 2 show the trade matrices of this region, one for individual economies, and the other a consolidated table. Economies are listed not in alphabetical order, but grouped together by geographical proximity because it provides us with a clear overview of the trade pattern of the region. They include Japan, China, East Asia 3 (South Korea, Hong Kong, and Chinese Taipei), ASEAN 7 (Brunei, Indonesia, Malaysia, the Philippines, Singapore, Thailand, and Vienam), Oceania (Australia, New Zealand, Papua New Guinea), the United States and America 4 (Canada, Chile, Mexico, Peru), and Russia. It also gives figures for APEC 21 and EU 15 for comparison. The European Union figures include trade among fifteen EU members.[9] The three years, 1995, 2001, and 2007, are selected as benchmarks for a long-term trend.

Exports and Imports of Major Groups

The extreme right-hand column of the trade matrix in Table 1 of the Appendix gives the total exports of individual economies and groups to the world, while the bottom row gives their total imports from the world. Its diagonal cells give the intraregional trade for groups, but zero for single economies such as Japan, China, the United States, and Russia. The trade matrix provides us with a lot of information and we will examine the size of trade, the intraregional trade ratio, the increase of trade, and trade intensity.

In East Asia, Japan and East Asia 3 exported about the same amount, followed by ASEAN 7 with its three quarters and China with its one third

TABLE 2.2
APEC's Three Activities

Liberalization
Osaka Action Agenda
Tariffs
Non-Tariff Measures
Services
Investment

Early Voluntary Sectoral Liberalization

Facilitation
Osaka Action Agenda
Standard and Conformance
Customs Procedure
Intellectual Property Rights
Government Procurement
Deregulation
Competition Policy
Rule of Origins
Dispute Settlement
Business Mobility
Implementation of the Uruguay Round Agreements

Economic and Technical Cooperation
Developing human capital
Developing stable and efficient markets through structural reform
Strengthening economic infrastructure
Facilitating technology flows and harnassing technologies for the future
Safeguarding the quality of life through environmentaly sound growth
Developing and strengthening the dynamism of SMEs
Integration into the global economy
Human security and counterterrorism
Promoting the development of knowledge-based economies
Addressing social dimension of globalization

in 1995. However, in 2007 China came up top, followed by East Asia 3, and ASEAN 7, all far exceeding Japan. A similar trend is witnessed in imports as well. Let us compare the whole of East Asia with America 5 (America 4 and the United States) and EU 15. EU 15 exported the largest amount, followed by East Asia with 57 per cent of this and America with

TABLE 2.3
Exports and Imports of Major Groups (billion U.S. dollars)

	To the world		From the world	
	1995	**2007**	**1995**	**2007**
Japan	443	714	335	563
China	148	1,218	129	843
East Asia 3	420	955	421	937
ASEAN 7	322	858	357	746
East Asia Total	1,335	3,547	1,243	3,094
America	847	1,948	1,003	2,520
EU 15	2,351	4,801	2,012	4,865

Source: Compiled from Appendix Table 2.

37 per cent. A similar ranking is observed in imports as well, with East Asia registering 62 per cent and America 5 registering 52 per cent of the EU 15 figures. As we saw in Chapter 1, EU 15 and America 5 have about the same GDP and East Asia has two thirds of this sum. The trade/GDP ratios, measuring the openness of the group's economy, is half that of America 5, but the same as that of EU 15.

Intraregional Trade Ratios

Let us compare the intraregional trade ratios of the three groups. The ratio is obtained by dividing the intraregional group trade by the average of its exports and imports. The European Union has the highest ratio of 60 per cent, but that of East Asia increased closer to the ratio of EU 15. Here it is worthwhile to mention the unique roles of Singapore and Hong Kong within East Asia. The percentage of Singapore's within intra-ASEAN 7 trade and that of Hong Kong within East Asia 3 and China, were 64 per cent and 67 per cent respectively, almost two thirds of the total group trade, in 2007.[10]

Trend of Trade Expansion

Let us review the trend of trade expansion. Appendix Table 3 gives the percentage rate of increase in 1995–2001 and 2001–07 of the individual economies in the Consolidated Trade matrix (Appendix Table 2). The extreme right-hand bottom cell gives the rate of increase of total world trade as 20 per cent for 1995–2001 and 123 per cent for 2001–07. Major groups' total exports in the right-hand columns and their total imports in the bottom rows give small or negative percentages for the first period, but very high percentages (more than double for half the groups) for the second period. Individually, China achieved distinguished growth in both periods, Russia decreased in the first, but recovered greatly in the second period, America 4 kept a similar growth rate in both periods, in both exports and imports.

The three years in Appendix 1 and 2 were given in order to obtain the average trend over a period brought upside down by the Asian currency crisis in 1997–98 and the Lehman shock in 2008–09. But ASEAN economies had not recovered fully from the currency crisis in 2009, while industrialized economies suffered from the bursting of the IT bubble, both falling far below the average trend in 2001. Thus the 1995–2001 rate tended to underestimate the trend for the first period, while the 2001–07 rate tended to overestimate that of the second period. However, it is worthwhile to note that we had a rapid expansion of trade before the Lehman shock.

Looking at the individual cells in Table 2.3, we can find which economies achieved higher trade expansion. The increase in the world total gives an average and can be used as a reference. China achieved a higher expansion in both exports and imports than any other economy, far exceeding the world average. The highest export expansion was China's exports to Russia, America 4, the European Union, Oceania, and ASEAN, while for its imports the highest expansion was from America 4, ASEAN, and Oceania. Russia's trade decreased for both exports and imports due to the change of political and economic regime in the first period, but both recovered greatly in the second period, as evidenced in her trade with East Asia 3, the European Union, China, Japan, and America 4.

Next comes ASEAN 7 for both exports and imports. Distinct expansion is witnessed in her exports to China, Russia, Oceania, while for imports, expansion was seen from China, America 4, and the intraregional trade of ASEAN 7 itself. East Asia 3's trade expansion was half of the average of the world total for the first period, but it picked up greatly for the second period.

Trade expansion of Japan and EU 15 was below the world average for both exports and imports. U.S. expansion in exports and imports exceeded the world average in the first period, but decelerated down to half of it in the second period. Oceania's expansion was closer to the world average among the industrialized economy groups, but increased for the trade with China, ASEAN, and Russia.

Trade Intensity Index

Trade intensity indices are taken from Appendix Tables 4 and 5. While values of trade in the trade matrix reflect the size of exporting and importing economies, the trade intensity index excludes the impact of size. This index is obtained by dividing the importer *j*'s share in the total export of exporter *i*, by *j*'s share in world imports. As the denominator reflects *j*'s size, if *i* exports in the same proportion, the intensity of *i* export to *j* will be 1. The intensity below 1 indicates a thin trade, while that above 1 gives close trade. On the other hand, the intensity of *j*'s export to *i* tends to give a similar intensity to that of *i* to *j*, but a different direction sometimes.

The trade intensity index in all diagonal cells are high (Appendix Table 5); 7–8 for Oceania, 3–4 for ASEAN, and 2 for East Asia. It is as low as 0.5 for America 4, which reflects the inclusion of four economies in a remote geographical location. The trade intensity for the United States and America 4 is as high as 5–7, while the trade intensity for APEC 21 is 1.5, close to that of the EU 15.

The trade intensities between Japan, China, East Asia 3, and ASEAN 7 are as high as 1.5–3, but they tend to decrease in the second period, except for the increasing intensity from 1 to 1.5 between China and ASEAN. Oceania shows high intensity with East Asian groups, reflecting its big

TABLE 2.4
Intraregional Trade Ratios

	East Asia	America 5	EU 15	APEC 21*
1995	50.6	43.8	63.5	72.2
2001	51.6	49.3	60.1	72.6
2007	57.7	44.3	58.9	68.6

Note: * Intraregional trade ratio depends not only on the trade intensity within the region but also the size of the region. Thus the intraregional trade ratio for APEC 21 has the biggest value because of its size, as it includes America and Russia.

Source: Calculated from Appendix Table 2 by (intraregional trade × 2)/(export to the world + imports from the world).

supply of primary products to East Asian groups. The United States has a high trade intensity of 1–1.5 with East Asian groups. China and the United States increased distinctly their intensity with each other. On the other hand, America 4's intensity with East Asian groups was as low as below 0.5. EU 15 has as low an intensity as below 0.5 with APEC economies except with Russia. Russia distinctly increased its intensity with the European Union but its trade intensity with APEC economies is low except for trade with China and Japan, reflecting its geographical location, that is the European part is much greater than its Asian part. To conclude, China led the world trade expansion, increasing her trade intensity with all groups, except Japan and East Asia, with which it traditionally already has high trade intensity.

Services and Direct Investment

We have so far only looked at commodity trade expansion, but a similar pattern is observed in services trade and outward and inward direct investments as well. The available statistics for services trade cover only cross-border transactions such as transportation of commodities and personnel, harbour and port services, business services, patent and royalty payment, and consumption abroad, all recorded in balance of payments statistics, which are classified as mode 1 and 2 in GATS (General Agreement on Trade in Services).

The services trade of all APEC economies amounted to 20 per cent of commodity trade in 2007. However, for 1995–2007, services exports grew by 184 per cent, much higher than the 140 per cent of commodity exports, while services imports grew at about 120 per cent, which is similar to the growth in commodity imports. Both the United States and Hong Kong had big surpluses, while other economies, including Japan, South Korea, Canada, and Mexico incurred deficits, leaving the whole of APEC almost balanced, unlike in commodity trade.

Outward and inward direct investments corresponded to "commercial presence" (Mode 3) in GATS typology. Outward and inward investments amounted to 11 per cent of commodity export and import respectively in 2007, and about half of services trade, but they grew by 270 per cent in both directions for 1995–2007, much higher than that in goods and services. Japan, South Korea, Chinese Taipei, and Russia were net outward investors, while China, Canada, Singapore, Thailand, and

Mexico were net (inward) recipients. The United States showed the biggest growth in both outward and inward investments, which amounted to 49 per cent and 36 per cent of the APEC total respectively, followed by Japan (11 per cent), Hong Kong, and Canada (each with 8 per cent) in outward investments. Personnel movement (mode 4 in GATS) seems to have accelerated as well, but no consistent statistics are available for all APEC economies.

Distinct Tendency of Globalization

The growth of international transactions is related to that of domestic activities. Appendix Table 6 gives the ratios of commodity export and import, services export and import, outward and inward direct investment to GDP for individual APEC economies in 1995, 2001, and 2007. The ratio of commodity trade with GDP is also called "trade dependence", which tends to be higher for small economies, reflecting their greater need for cross-border transactions; 120–140 per cent for Singapore and Hong Kong, 80 per cent for Malaysia, 50–70 per cent for PNG, Brunei, Chinese Taipei, Vietnam, and Thailand, and 30–40 per cent for Canada, South Korea, and the Philippines. On the other hand, this ratio is about 10 per cent for Japan and Australia, and less than 10 per cent for the United States.

It is worthwhile to note that in spite of her big size, China's export and import dependence amounted to as high as 35 per cent and 24 per cent respectively in 2007. This reflects the openness of the economy and the incorporation of international transactions in the domestic economy. Trade dependence increased in all economies for the period 1995–2007, reflecting increasing globalization. This trend is most distinct in China, South Korea, Chinese Taipei, Thailand, Vietnam, Canada, Chile, and Peru. It increased by 50 per cent from 14 per cent to 21 per cent for APEC as a whole. EU 15 led in this trend, from 26 per cent to 30 per cent in exports, and from 23 per cent to 31 per cent in imports.

The figures for the services trade are smaller because they amounted to only 20 per cent of the commodity trade, and were 20–40 per cent for Singapore and Hong Kong, 10 per cent level for Malaysia, Thailand, PNG, 2–3 per cent for China, Japan, and the United States. Here too, many economies increased this ratio, especially in South Korea, Thailand, and Vietnam.

The ratio of direct investments to GDP was lower, but showed a similar pattern to that for goods and services. Dependence on inward investments was as high as 28 per cent for Hong Kong and 24 per cent for China, followed by Singapore, Canada, Vietnam, Malaysia, Chile, and Peru. Dependence on outward investment was as high as 25 per cent for Hong Kong, followed by Singapore, China, Malaysia, and Canada. EU 15 was active in both outward and inward investment and increased its ratio to GDP above that of the APEC average.

We have so far seen that commodity trade, services trade, and direct investment expanded in APEC economies from 1995 to 2007, especially in the 2000s. This is most distinguished in China, Hong Kong, Singapore, and Vietnam, reflecting their high growth pattern. It is difficult to regress this growth on APEC's programme of liberalization and facilitation. Few academic studies have ever succeeded in identifying trade and investment expansion by a particular policy measure on an ex-post basis. However, it is evident from our statistics that the developing economies of APEC have expanded trade and investment more than the European Union and their GDP ratios increased as globalization progressed. As we will see in Chapter 4, these economies still keep trade and investment barriers but they have *made the remarkable growth in spite of the remaining barriers.* Can we then not claim that APEC's policy coordination of liberalization and facilitation has worked well in the APEC region?

Notes

1. The main theme of the first PAFTAD conference was "Pacific Free Trade Area" (PFTA) proposed by Kojima. Concerned about the Pacific economies being left behind with the development of the EEC, he urged the reduction of tariff barriers among the five advanced Pacific economies and expansion of trade across the Pacific, but met the reservation by some participants who argued that it would aggravate the imbalance of trade between member economies. There was no follow-up to this issue in the succeeding conference except for the discussion of the Pacific Payment Clearing Union. The PFTD conference series has picked up such issues as macroeconomic policy, trade, domestic adjustment, technical transfer, and development cooperation common to participating economies, and enhanced mutual understanding in the region.
2. The failure of EVSL resulted from attempts to reduce tariffs and NTMs in the "not easy" sectors, which had the highest resistance to liberalization, such as forestry and fish products, in the WTO formula (Yamazawa and Urata 2000).
3. This point was made by a few academic attempts at assessing IAPs/CAPs

even in their early years. Yamazawa and Urata (2000) and Feinberg and Zhan (2001).

4. This implies a looser economic integration than ordinary FTAs, and Andrew Elek and I named it Open Economic Association, but unfortunately the term was not widespread (Yamazawa 1992).
5. Learned from Yoichi Suzuki, who was in charge of drafting the Osaka Action Agenda in 1994–95 on 13 January 2010. Apparently some economies were disappointed with this weak modality of liberalization set in the Osaka Action Agenda (1995), the small liberalization package committed in the IAPs (1997), and the failure of EVSL (1998). As New Zealand hosted APEC in 1999, the like-minded economies continued their path-finding talks for further liberalization within APEC, which was realized in the form of a TPP (Trans-Pacific Strategic Partnership) Agreement in 2005. Refer to Chapter 6.
6. Soesastro (2006) in Drysdale and Terada, eds. (2006).
7. Soesastro (2009) in Kesavapany and Lim, eds. (2009).
8. Woo (2005) criticized this tendency of the IAP peer review report to follow the TPRM, and characterizing them as incomplete reports of the members' trade policies, insisting that individual IAPs should identify APEC's value-added. I also served as a consultant and share Woo's criticism of many of the review reports that followed the TPRM. However, it is too narrow an assessment of an individual economy's approach towards achieving the Bogor Goals to focus on just its APEC's value-added alone.
9. The European Union has expanded to twenty-seven members by now, but, in order to examine the expansion between 1995 and 2007, we applied the 1995 membership figure to 2001 and 2007.
10. These figures are taken from Appendix Table 1.

3

Organization and Activities of APEC

Unique Network for Intergovernmental Cooperation

APEC started as an annual meeting of foreign and trade ministers discussing economic cooperation in the Asia Pacific. However, after the Leaders' Meeting was added to it in 1993, it has been attracting media attention as a big event in which presidents and prime ministers of major economies in the Asia-Pacific gather once a year. Their discussion shifted to the liberalization of trade and investment as well. Participating economies have taken turns every year in hosting the Leaders' and Ministerial Meetings in October or November, and taking the initiative in the whole APEC activities. Senior officials of all participating economies meet three to four times a year and consult one another on the preparation for the two meetings. Additionally, committees and taskforces are organized by officials in charge of individual areas and issues. APEC has now become a busy working framework for intergovernmental cooperation all year round. This modality of consultation has evolved while APEC followed its precedent PECC (Pacific Economic Cooperation Council) both in membership, agenda setting, and modality of cooperation. Figure 3.1 shows APEC's organization, which has evolved over several years.

Ministerial meetings are organized for sixteen individual areas besides the two main meetings (Ministerial Meeting and Leaders' Meeting) at irregular intervals (Table 3.1). Three meetings in charge of finance, trade,

FIGURE 3.1
Organization of APEC (as of 2010)

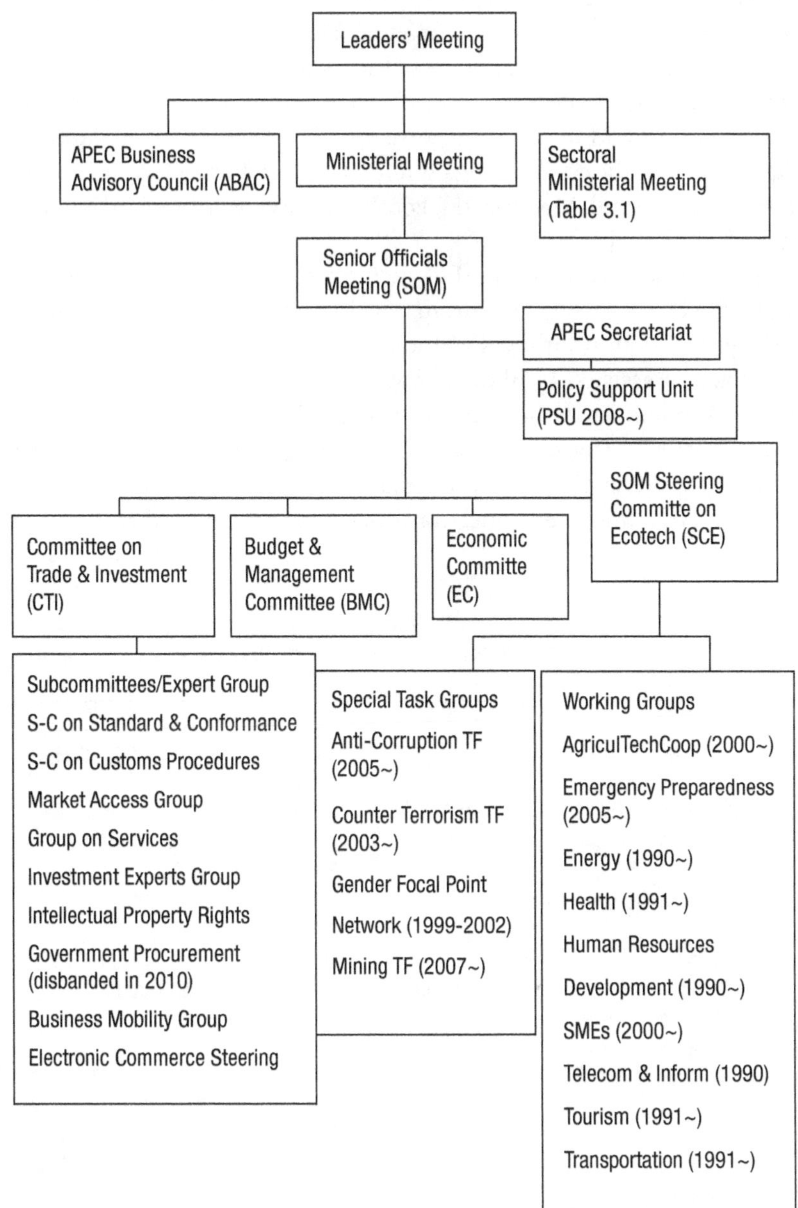
Leaders' Meeting
APEC Business Advisory Council (ABAC)
Ministerial Meeting
Sectoral Ministerial Meeting (Table 3.1)
Senior Officials Meeting (SOM)
APEC Secretariat
Policy Support Unit (PSU 2008~)
SOM Steering Committe on Ecotech (SCE)
Committee on Trade & Investment (CTI)
Budget & Management Committee (BMC)
Economic Committe (EC)
Subcommittees/Expert Group
S-C on Standard & Conformance
S-C on Customs Procedures
Market Access Group
Group on Services
Investment Experts Group
Intellectual Property Rights
Government Procurement (disbanded in 2010)
Business Mobility Group
Electronic Commerce Steering
Special Task Groups
Anti-Corruption TF (2005~)
Counter Terrorism TF (2003~)
Gender Focal Point
Network (1999-2002)
Mining TF (2007~)
Working Groups
AgriculTechCoop (2000~)
Emergency Preparedness (2005~)
Energy (1990~)
Health (1991~)
Human Resources
Development (1990~)
SMEs (2000~)
Telecom & Inform (1990)
Tourism (1991~)
Transportation (1991~)

Source: APEC Secretariat's website.

and small and medium enterprises (SME) have been organized every year since 1994–96. The trade Ministers Meeting is usually held together with the second Senior Officials Meeting (SOM) in June, and provides the main setting for finalizing the year's agenda. The Finance Ministers Meeting used to be organized separately from the main meetings, but has begun to be organized just before them since 2008 when the G-20 Summit started on macroeconomic and financial cooperation. Besides the sixteen areas listed in Table 3.1, additional meetings will be held when needed. Incidentally, the first Ministerial Meeting on Food Security was held in Niigata in October 2010.

The SOMs are a core of APEC activities. Two senior officials, at the deputy-director-general level from the Ministry of Foreign Affairs and Ministry of Economy, Trade and Industry respectively, represent Japan in SOM. Each is assisted by the chief and staff of the APEC Office in their respective ministries. Other ministries, including the Ministry of Finance and Cabinet Office (formerly Economic Planning Agency), dispatch director-level officials in charge of APEC-related issues. Other economies seem to be represented by similar personnel from governments so that APEC constitutes

TABLE 3.1
Sectoral Ministerial Meetings Held, 1992–2008

Education	1992, 2000, 2004, 2008
Energy	1996, 1997, 1998, 2000, 2002, 2004, 2005, 2007
Environment Sustainable Development	1994, 1996, 1997
Finance	1994 and annually
Health	2003, 2006, 2007
Human Resource Development	1996, 1997, 1999, 2001?
Mining	2004, 2005, 2007
Ocean-related	2002, 2005
Regional Science & Technology Cooperation	1995, 1996, 1998, 2004
Small and Medium Enterprises	1994 and annually
Structural Reform	2008
Telecommunications & Information	1995, 1996, 1998, 2000, 2002, 2005, 2008
Trade	1994, and annually from 1996
Transportation	1995, 1997, 2002, 2004, 2007, 2009
Women's Affairs	1998, 2002
Tourism	2000, 2002, 2004, 2006, 2008

Source: APEC Secretariat's website.

a big framework for intergovernmental cooperation on a variety of issues. In addition, a small permanent secretariat is located in Singapore and assists SOM and committees.

Thus APEC has already developed from merely an annual conference series to a permanent institution for intergovernmental consultation, covering a vast area of regional cooperation. Let me compare it with the European Union, a highly institutionalized organization for regional integration. How does the European Union secure the market integration for its almost completed single market?

The European Union's single market is based on the freedom of movement of people, goods, services, and capital, and eliminates all barriers to their movements.[1] It is legally founded on the treaty establishing the European Community. Its Internal Market Directives lists the following legislation in force: internal market, free movement of people, free movement of workers, free movement of goods, the right of establishment and freedom to provide services, free movement of capital, laws relating to undertakings, and public contracts.

It is vital that member states adopt these laws both on time and correctly. They need to be transposed to their individual members' domestic legislation. The European Union checks on them and points out any infringement, and publishes the transposition deficit (the percentage of laws not correctly transposed) in the annual *Internal Market Scoreboard* report. Its 2009 report shows that the European Union's average transposition deficit was 1 per cent for the third consecutive time.[2] Eighteen out of twenty-seven member states are in line with the 1 per cent target. And three member states have achieved an almost perfect score. On the other hand, seven member states are far off the target and six of them have worsened, which has generated serious concern. The names of these member states are all published in the report.

APEC, with its modality based on voluntariness and which is non-binding, does not have enforcing power like the European Union so its integration measures are not adopted as laws and member economies are not singled out for infringement. At most, all member economies agree on the measures benefiting all members and announce them, as in the case of non-binding principles in foreign investment, customs procedures, and government procurement. Individual economies accept them voluntarily because they benefit from them. In cases where some economies lag behind in implementation due to the lack of legal capacity, the Collective

Action Plan (CAP) provides the necessary technical assistance from the advanced economies. As we saw in the previous chapter, APEC has introduced the "Peer Review Process", a delicate element in urging economies to advance difficult issues such as liberalization, although it never presents the economies as failing to implement them. Nevertheless, APEC has made good progress in the facilitation areas as we will see in the next chapter. This is partly because facilitation could proceed under the non-binding principles and partly because APEC's intergovernmental consultation has worked effectively.

Committees and Task Forces

Let me continue to explain the workings of the APEC organization. The Committee for Trade and Investment (CTI) oversees APEC's major activity, which is trade investment liberalization and facilitation (TILF), assisted by subcommittees or expert groups in charge of nine areas under it (Figure 3.1). They cover almost all individual areas in the Osaka Action Agenda. Each subcommittee or expert group manages the implementation of the CAP in its own area.

Another major activity, Ecotech, is overseen by the Sub-Committee on Ecotech under SOM (SCE). SCE has twelve working groups, most of which have been in existence since the start of APEC (Table 1.3), and added four special task forces in the 2000s to take charge of the new agenda of APEC. The progress and achievement of working groups and special task forces depend upon the initiative of their chairs/convenors. Participants in individual Ecotech projects come from individual economy governments, are private sector specialists commissioned by individual governments, academics, and non-governmental organizations who have strong interest in the project. The last group is sometimes eager to promote regional cooperation in particular issues rather than APEC itself, but nevertheless they are important stakeholders of APEC.

The Economic Committee used to conduct economic analyses and publish academic reports on macroeconomic analyses. However, it was reorganized in 2006 and assigned structural reform, a new agenda of APEC (see Chapter 5 for further details). The Budget and Management Committee oversees APEC's central fund, which is, however, limited. APEC's central fund budget started with US$3.3 million contributed annually by participating economies, but was increased by 30 per cent to

US$5 million in 2009.[3] It is spent on the secretariat's activities and various projects mentioned above. APEC member economies also often voluntarily provide funds for carrying out projects to advance APEC's agenda. For example, Japan has contributed US$1.6 to US$4.6 million to TILF-related projects every year since 1997. Ecotech projects are also financially supported by the particular economies which proposed the projects. Expenditures on organizing official meetings are paid for by the organizing economies, and participants pay their own expenses in principle. Travel expenses for participants to APEC-funded projects from developing economies are often borne by the APEC fund.

APEC Secretariat

During its first decade, APEC host economies served as its secretariat in the preparation for organizing the Leaders' and Ministerial Meetings. This changed when a permanent secretariat was established in Singapore in 1993. It had a small office occupying only two floors of a tall, pencil-shaped building provided by the Government of Singapore, but has now moved to its present office occupying an independent building next to the campus of the National University of Singapore in 2003.

One or two officials are dispatched here from the major economies, usually for a three-year term each. They are young career officials of ministries of foreign affairs or trade, and work as directors assisting SOM, committees/working groups, or specific areas, such as the peer-review process of the Individual Action Plans (IAPs), drafting reports for chairs of subcommittees and working groups. Assistants for helping directors are mostly recruited in Singapore.[4] Incidentally, English is the *de facto* official language in APEC, spoken at all meetings and all reports are published in English. Although it is not the native language in more than half the twenty-one APEC economies, English is accepted as the de facto language for practical reasons. The cost will be tremendous if APEC were to publish reports in all the languages of the participating economies like the European Union does!

The executive director, head of the APEC Secretariat, is dispatched from an economy hosting APEC in a particular year, while the deputy executive director is from the next host economy, so there is close communication between the secretariat and host economies. It was pointed out that both the small size of the secretariat relative to APEC's activities, and the frequent change of secretary general and his deputy had tended to constrain the secretariat's activities and that the secretariat needs to be enlarged and strengthened. Initially, Asian members had preferred to keep the secretariat as small as possible and agreed to only a small increase in the number of directors.

However, APEC member economies decided in 2007 to strengthen the secretariat. A fixed-term executive director has been appointed, independent of host economies, starting from 2010. The Policy Support Unit, which provides APEC member economies with research, analyses, and policy suggestions, was established with around ten professional staff in 2008.

The APEC Secretariat also takes care of publishing and disseminating APEC's achievements. Every year APEC publishes the Leaders' Declaration, Joint Ministerial Statement, proceedings of major meetings and task forces, and puts them on its website in near real time for anybody interested. The APEC Secretariat also commissions research and studies from private sector think tanks. In the IAP peer review process, it commissions consultants to produce review reports. Peer review reports are submitted for further discussion at SOM's special sessions and are made public on the APEC Secretariat's website.

Business Participation: APEC Business Advisory Council

APEC is a governmental institution and constituted mainly by officials. However, since it is interlinked with private sector economic activities, it is imperative that it acquires knowledge, information, and cooperation from the private sector. In 1993 the APEC Ministerial Meeting established two advisory committees: the Eminent Persons Group (EPG) and the Pacific Business Forum (PBF).

The EPG was constituted by one private individual from each economy and chaired by Fred Bergsten of the United States. It was never an academic group. Academics constituted only a third of the group,while a variety of professions constituted the group, including former politicians, former government officials, businessmen, and journalists. A few business participants of this group later joined the APEC Business Advisory Council

(ABAC) and took the initiative in making recommendations to the leaders. In August 1993 the EPG submitted its first report, *A Vision for APEC: Towards an Asia Pacific Economic Community* (APEC/EPG 1993) and affected the basic direction of the first Leaders' Declaration in November. The EPG continued to make proposals, focusing on trade and investment liberalization, such as the timetable for liberalization beyond the Uruguay Round, and open subregionalism, in its second and third reports. The reports also included APEC's dispute mediation services, and monetary and macroeconomic cooperation.[5]

On the other hand, the business advisory council PBF was engaged in APEC differently. APEC expected from the PBF not so much its vision proposal, but rather its encouragement of private firms' participation in APEC activities, and closer private–government cooperation. PBF was constituted by two members from each economy and submitted two reports, but its proposal was more concrete and reflected the interests of the business sector (Tommy Koh, Lee Tsao Yun, and Arun Mahizhnan 2009).

After EPG was disbanded in 1995, PBF was enlarged and reorganized to the ABAC, with three participants from each economy, including one representing small and medium enterprises. ABAC is expected to advise on APEC's work programmes, while conveying the priorities of the business sector and related information. The first ABAC report submitted in October 1996 included a variety of recommendations linking business with APEC, such as the APEC Business Visa, APEC Voluntary Investment Projects for furthering infrastructure investment, and a roundtable for private-government cooperation on infrastructure investment (ABAC 1996). The host of APEC in 1996, President Ramos, coined the catch phrase "APEC is business", and invited hundreds of foreign businessmen and investors to the Manila APEC to encourage them to invest in the Philippines. He initiated a dialogue series between APEC leaders and business representatives, which has since become a regular event of ABAC.

ABAC submits recommendations to APEC leaders every year. Table 3.2 lists the titles of ABAC's recommendations from 1996 to 2010. In fact, ABAC reviews APEC work programmes in individual areas and indicates business priority, but the titles in this table also convey the shift of business priorities over the past fifteen years, such as capacity building for globalization in 2000, strengthening security in 2002, and fair growth and harmonious community since 2003.

TABLE 3.2
ABAC Reports to APEC Leaders

1996:	APEC Means Business: Building Prosperity for our Community
1997:	APEC Means Business: ABAC's Call to Action
1998:	APEC Means Business: Restoring Confidence, Regenerating Growth
1999:	(no title)
2000:	Facing Globalization the APEC Way
2001:	Common Development through Market Opening, Capacity Building and Full Participation
2002:	Sharing: Development to Reinforce Global Security
2003:	Harmony in Diversity: Achieving Balanced and Equitable Growth
2004:	Bridging the Pacific: Coping with the Challenges of Globalization
2005:	Networking Asia-Pacific: A Pathway to Common Prosperity
2006:	Driving Forward a Prosperous and Harmonized APEC Community
2007:	ABAC Interaction and Cooperation with APEC
2008:	Mind the Gap: Making Globalization an Opportunity for All
2009:	Building Towards the Bogor Goals with One Community
2010:	Working towards Sustainable Growth for All

Source: Support Council for ABAC Japan.

ABAC has also made several recommendations which were actually implemented by APEC and regarded as its achievements: the APEC Business Travel Card (ABTC) in 1996, a study proposal of a Free Trade Area of the Asia-Pacific (FTAAP) in 2006, and suggestions for the stability of the financial system and fostering the bond market in 2007. ABAC also organizes industry dialogues in such strategic areas as automobiles, chemistry, agricultural biotech, life science innovation.

Despite this, ABAC has complained that APEC has not responded well to their recommendations and it has proposed an official feedback mechanism in which APEC's executive director reports regularly to ABAC members on APEC's responses to their recommendations (ABAC 2002). ABAC also wishes to have regular contact with APEC not only at the leaders, ministerial, and SOM levels, but also at the committee and subcommittee levels (ABAC 2007). In response to these demands, APEC now invites all ABAC members to APEC's main meetings and organizes close dialogues between three to four leaders and several ABAC members. The business community of the host economy also organizes a big business forum, the CEO Summit, on the day preceding the Leaders' Meeting, and discusses the agenda for the year.

Other Activities of the Private Sector

The Asia Pacific community cannot be built only by governments of participating economies, but also needs contributions from other private bodies. Let us review these: the Pacific Economic Cooperation Council (PECC), Pacific Basin Economic Council (PBEC), Pacific Trade and Development Conference (PAFTAD), and APEC Study Center Consortium (ASCC). The first three had started much earlier than APEC itself and provided solid bases for APEC's development in the 1990s as explained in Chapter 2.

The PECC has been related closely with APEC as its semi-official predecessor of tripartite participation of business, academia, and government from twenty-five economies in the Asia Pacific. PECC representatives have been participating in the SOM and other committees and task force meetings as observers and it continues its occasional contributions to APEC activities. PECC organizes a general assembly every other year, while the International Steering Committee and Coordinating Group, with representatives from each participating economy manages its activities. A small permanent secretariat was set up in Singapore in the mid-1980s. Staffed with a professional director general and five or six experts it oversees the activities of sixteen taskforces. This resembles the organization of APEC, but the fact is that APEC has followed PECC in implementing its activities and expanding its membership. For a decade before APEC started, PECC served partly as a network of semi-official consultation. The president or prime minister of a host economy used to address it at its general assembly, while former ministers and ambassadors are now represented in the International Steering Committee. PECC currently has twenty-five participating economies — all twenty-one APEC member economies, plus Colombia, Mongolia, the French Pacific Islands, and the South Pacific Islands Forum. Each has its national committee, headed by its Steering Committee member.

The PECC's task forces include the Pacific Economic Outlook; Trade Policy Forum; Mineral and Energy Forum; Financial Market Development; Food and Agriculture; Fishery; Science and Technology; Telecommunication, Transportation, and Tourism (3T); and Pacific Islands, covering vast areas of regional cooperation. Each task force is typically led by its coordinator, who is usually dispatched by the proponent economy. It conducts a policy-oriented study and survey on various issues of regional cooperation in the Asia Pacific, discusses its results at forum meetings, and submits a report to participating governments. These activities are now being carried out directly by APEC and official financial support for PECC has been squeezed since APEC started, so much so that PECC's activities have now decreased except for biannual assembly meetings.

The PBEC also has observer status in APEC, but has engaged with APEC in a different way to that of the PECC. The PBEC was established by business organizations in major Asia-Pacific economies, independently from their governments. It used to organize a big conference annually somewhere in the Asia-Pacific and encouraged business interest in cooperation of the Pacific region. However, its activity seems to have been shared by ABAC in recent years.

PAFTAD is a voluntary organization of academic economists with a keen interest in cooperation in the Pacific. It has continued its discussion of policy-oriented studies for the past forty years. Regular participants from thirteen to fourteen economies constitute a steering committee and organize an international conference every eighteen months on a particular economic issue for Asia-Pacific cooperation. In June 1999, I organized its 25th conference in Osaka, in which it reviewed the achievements of APEC in its first decade, and discussed its future development, covering trade policy, macroeconomic policy, economic cooperation, and industrial policies of the automobile industry, IT, and agriculture, as well as competition policy (Yamazawa 2000). PAFTAD economists also participate in PECC activities and help ABAC in conducting research related to its recommendations.[6]

The APEC Study Center Consortium (ASCC) is a new face started by the suggestion of the need for wider academic support for APEC in the first Leaders' Statement in Seattle in 1993. Universities and research institutes are designated as APEC study centres in many APEC economies. Each has established a study unit for APEC-related research and dispatches researchers to an annual meeting of the ASCC, organized by the APEC host economy of the year. Although officially acknowledged as part of APEC, government support differs greatly among the economies so that only a few ASC national consortiums have continued systematic research activities.

Notes

1. The information here is based on the European Commission's website on Internal Market: General Policy Framework at <http://ec.surope.eu/internal_market/top_layer/index_1_en.htm>.
2. EC, *Internal Market Scoreboard*, July 2009, also downloaded from the website indicated in note 1.
3. APEC Secretariat's website.
4. Please refer to Hattori (2009) for concrete details of the activities of APEC secretariats. He was dispatched from METI (Ministry of Economy, Trade and Industry) and worked there from 2006 to 2008.
5. Chapter 2 explains how the EPG reports affected APEC's strategy for liberalization in 1993–95.
6. PAFTAD was originally proposed by Kiyoshi Kojima and Saburo Ohkita, both from Japan, and they served as the first and second chair of its steering committee. After 1993 Hugh Patrick of the United States, another founding member, served as the third chair. Peter Drysdale of the Australian National University has been serving at its international secretariat since the 1970s.

4

Has APEC Achieved the Mid-term Bogor Goals?

The Year of Mid-term Bogor Goal

The year 2010 was the mid-term target of the Bogor Goals issued by President Soeharto that "industrialized economies achieve free and open trade by the year 2010, while rest of the economies by 2020". Have these ambitious goals been achieved? Although it is not well known that APEC has shifted to more realistic timelines since the Asian currency crisis, many people still remember the Bogor Goals, APEC's main appeal. APEC has to reply to this question, which Japan, as its host in 2010, tackled together with senior officials of other economies. Japan's hosting of APEC this particular year may be related to the fact that she also hosted it and produced the Osaka Action Agenda to achieve the Bogor Goals in 1995.

It requires sensitive diplomatic efforts to respond to this question given APEC's "no name, no shame" modality. Despite such diplomatic constraint, economists wish to find out to what extent the Bogor Goals have been achieved so far. This chapter presents an attempt by an independent expert.[1]

At November's Leaders' Meeting and Ministerial Meeting in Japan, APEC provided an assessment of the progress towards achieving the Bogor Goals by the industrialized economies plus alpha.[2] APEC's IAPs

(Individual Action Plans) tend to give details of implementations in its positive list that stretches over hundreds of pages but seldom mentions what still remains unachieved. It is contrary to the European Union's formula in which all measures of regional integration are obligatory under the law, and the implementation by individual member states are scored openly so that they are effectively implemented (p. 28). APEC will not be able to adopt the European Union formula immediately, but the author believes that APEC needs to move in the direction of objective assessment of individual economy's achievements.

Quantitative Assessment: Methodology and Basic Data

Our quantitative assessment is made based on the IAP peer reviews and MTST (Mid-Term Stock-Take) Project Team Experts Report (2005). The latter provides the only comparative analysis of all APEC economies' progress towards the Bogor Goals in fifteen areas of the Osaka Action Agenda (OAA), based on the peer review reports of 2003–05. It was updated with the IAPs and Peer Review Reports of 2007–09. The peer review reports were adopted through discussions at SOM and it is quite legitimate to base our assessment on this information. In order to quantify our assessment, we have introduced a five-grade system as follows:

5: Almost achieved
4: Achieved with major exceptions
3: Achieved by more than half
2: Implemented partly
1: Not started yet.

Precise criteria for each grade are set for concrete stages of achievement in individual areas (Table 4.1). These may sound too broad a base for assessment, but they are the maximum we can claim as objective assessment, based on the IAP peer reviews and MTST reports.

Our assessment proceeded as follows:

(1) Specify the concrete details of the Bogor Goals by individual areas, according to the OAA. Draw a road map of five stages towards the goal, which provides us with the five grades in our assessment of achievement (Table 4.1)
(2) Assess individual economies' progress by area, score them based on the Peer Review Report and MTST expert report (Table 4.2), and produce a summary matrix of economies by area (Table 4.3).
(3) Draw a radar chart for each economy (Figures 4.1–4.21), which show

TABLE 4.1
Criteria for Five-grade Assessment by Area

Criteria for five grades:
5: Almost achieved, 4: Achieved with major exceptions, 3: Achieved by more than half, 2: Implemented partly, 1: Not started yet.

Tariffs	5	SAA tariffs of 5% or less and peak tariffs less than 5%
	4	SAA tariffs of 6–10% and peak tariffs less than 10%
	3	SAA tariffs of 11–20% and peak tariffs less than 20%
	2	SAA tariffs of over 20% and many peak tariffs
	1	
Services	5	Number of GATS liberalized sectors: 25–19
	4	Number of GATS liberalized sectors: 15–8
	3	Number of GATS liberalized sectors: less than 6
	2	No GATS sector committed yet
	1	
Investment	5	No pre-restrictions to FDI, EODB: 1–40
	4	No post-regulations of FDI, EODB: 41–80
	3	Protection of FDI, free redemption of profits; EODB: over 80
	2	FDI legislation
	1	
Standards & Conformance	5	Achieved a high level of international alignment, expanding MRA
	4	Adopted ISO and IEO, but starting MRA
	3	Achieved only partial international alignment
	2	Setting domestic standards and preparing administrative agencies
	1	
Customs Procedures	5	Adopted RKC and introduced the Single Window
	4	Preparing for RKC and the Single Window
	3	Adopted HSC, Valuation Agreement, UN/EDIFACT
	2	Preparing customs procedures
	1	
Intellectual Property Rights	5	Adopted the Paris Convention and WTO/TRIP
	4	Arranged legislation and administration enforcing IPR
	3	Adopted domestic legislation of patents, designs, and trademarks
	2	Preparing for IPR protection
	1	
Government Procurement	5	Ratified WTO/Government Purchase Agreement
	4	Implemented e-bidding and related facilities
	3	Preparing government purchase procedures
	2	
	1	
Business Visa	5	Effective implementation of ABTC or equivalent
	4	Published *ABTH* for short-term business trips and stays
	3	Arranged visa system and free access
	2	
	1	

TABLE 4.2
Basic Data for Five-grade Assessment

	SA applied Tariffs	SA bound Tariffs	Peak Tariffs	Services Number of Sectors in GATS Commitment Tables 2003: A–B–C* Number of Sectors committed under AFAS
Australia	3.5	9.9	0	25 – 30 – 0
Brunei	3.6	25.3	0.06	3 – 22 – 32 (AFAS 3)
Canada	5.5	6.5	0.27	15 – 26 – 14
Chile	6.0	25.1	0.14	2 – 25 – 28
China	9.9	10.0	6.14	14 – 33 – 8 Acceded to WTO/GATS in 2002
Hong Kong	0	0	0	4 – 38 – 13
Indonesia	6.9	37.1	2.65	6 – 26 – 23 (AFAS 16)
Japan	5.1	5.1	4.95	19 – 36 – 0
Republic of Korea	12.2	17.0	4.89	15 – 26 – 14
Malaysia	8.4	24.5	13.31	11 – 30 – 14 (AFAS 9)
Mexico	12.6	36.1	0.12	12 – 34 – 9
New Zealand	3.0	9.9	0	8 – 38 – 9
Papua New Guinea	5.3	32.4	n.a.	8 – 28 – 19
Peru	10.2	30.1	0	1 – 36 – 18
Philippines	6.3	25.6	2.38	4 – 23 – 28 (AFAS 8)
Russia	11.0	—	2.6	n.a. not acceded to WTO/GATS yet
Singapore	0	12.1	0	10 – 27 – 8 (AFAS 18)
Chinese Taipei	5.6	6.4	3.26	20 – 35 – 0
Thailand	10.0	28.1	19.5	2 – 49 – 4 (AFAS 23)
United States	3.5	3.5	2.89	25 – 30 – 0
Vietnam	16.8	11.4	20.66	9 – 46 – 0 Acceded to WTO/GATS in 2006

a line connecting scores of achievement in individual areas, that is, the current pattern of the economy's level of achievement of the Bogor Goals. The outermost line connecting the score 5 for all areas shows that the economy has achieved the Bogor Goals. The dotted line connecting the average scores of twenty-one APEC economies is also provided in each radar chart so that we can compare the economy's achievement with the APEC average.

The IAPs and MTST reports convey huge amounts of information on individual economies' progress using the positive list formula, which is not easily readable. The advantage of our quantitative assessment is to

TABLE 4.2 — *cont'd*

	Investment (EODB index)	Standard & Conformance (international alignment %)	Customs Procedure
Australia	Stage A, Group III, 9	ISO, IEC, VAP, 80%	RKC adop'd, SW in prep 3.58
Brunei	Stage B, 88	VAP	—
Canada	Stage A, Group III, 8	ISO, IEC, VAP 70%	RKC adop'd, SW impl'd 3.82
Chile	Stage A, Group III, 40	ISO	SW impl'd 3.32
China	Stage C, Group I, 83	ISO, IEC, VAP 44%	RKC adop'd, SW impl'd 2.99
Hong Kong	Stage A, Group III, 4	VAP	3.84
Indonesia	Stage C, Group II, 129	ISO, IEC, VAP	RKC adop'd partly 2.73
Japan	Stage A, Group III, 12	ISO, IEC, VAP High alignment	RKC adop'd, SW impl'd 3.79
South Korea	Stage A, Group III, 23	ISO, IEC 99%	RKC adop'd, SW impl'd 3.22
Malaysia	Stage B, Group II, 20	ISO, IEC, VAP 50%	RKC adop'd 3.36
Mexico	Stage B, Group II, 56	ISO, IEC 66%	2.5
New Zealand	Stage A, Group III, 2	ISO, IEC, VAP, Alignment completed	RKC adop'd SW in prep 3.57
PNG	Stage C, 95	ISO, IEC, Codex	RKC adop'd partly 2
Peru	Stage B, Group II, 62	ISO, IEC 15%	RKC adop'd partly SW in prep 2.68
The Philippines	Stage C, Group II, 140	ISO, IEC, VAP 77%	RKC adop'd partly SW in prep 2.64
Russia	Stage C, Group I, 120	ISO, IEC	SW in prep 1.94
Singapore	Stage A, Group III, 1	ISO, IEC, VAP	SW impl'd 3.9
Chinese Taipei	Stage B, Group III, 61	VAP Alignment completed	SW in prep 3.25
Thailand	Stage B, Group II, 13	ISO, IEC, VAP 25%	RKC adop'd partly SW in prep 3.03
United States	Stage A, Group III, 3	ISO, IEC, VAP High alignment	RKC adop'd SW in prep 3.52
Vietnam	Stage C, Group I, 92	ISO, IEC, VAP 24%	RKC adop'd SW in prep 2.89

	Intellectual Property Rights	Government Procurement	Business Mobility
Australia	Paris Convention & TRIP	Agreement with NZ	ABTH, ABTC
Brunei	Own rule consistent with WIPO/TRIP	Domestic rule, equivalent with others	ABTH, ABTC
Canada	Paris Conventiion & TRIP	GPA adopted	ABTH, ABTC prov'l
Chile	Paris Convention & TRIP	e-bidding introduced	ABTH, ABTC
China	Paris Convention & TRIP	GPA preparing	ABTH, ABTC

continued on next page

TABLE 4.2 — *cont'd*

	Intellectual Property Rights	Government Procurement	Business Mobility
Hong Kong	Paris Convention & TRIP	GPA adopted	ABTH, ABTC
Indonesia	Paris Convention & TRIP	Legislation arranged	ABTH, ABTC
Japan	Paris Convention & TRIP	GPA adopted	ABTH, ABTC
South Korea	Paris Convention & TRIP	GPA adopted	ABTH, ABTC
Malaysia	Enforcement arranged	e-bidding implemented	ABTH, ABTC
Mexico	Enforcement arranged	Legislation arranged	ABTH, ABTC
New Zealand	Paris Convention & TRIP	Agreement with Australia	ABTH, ABTC
PNG	legislation, TRIP	Handled by CSTB	ABTH, ABTC
Peru	Enforcement arranged	e-bidding introduced	ABTH, ABTC
The Philippines	Legislation arranged	Legislation arranged	ABTH, ABTC
Russia	Legislation arranged	Federal legislation amended 2007	ABTH
Singapore	Paris Convention & TRIP	GPA adopted, NBP consistent	ABTH, ABTC
Chinese Taipei	Paris Convention	NBP consistent	ABTH, ABTC
Thailand	Paris Convention & TRIP	Legislation arranged	ABTH, ABTC
United States	Paris Convention & TRIP	GPA adopted	ABTH, ABTC prov'l
Vietnam	Preparing Legislation	Preparing GP rules	ABTH, ABTC

Annotations to Table 4.2

Tariffs: Simple average applied tariffs, simple average WTO-bound tariffs, and percentage of peak tariffs in total tariff lines. SAB tariffs are only for reference. *Sources: SAA and SAB tariffs from World Tariff Profiles, country pages and peak tariffs from IAPs.*

Services: A-B-C denote the number of sectors (total 55) "bound", "unbound", and "not stated" for market access, and/or national treatment in both Mode 1 and Mode 3 in GATS Commitment Tables 2003. The numbers in parentheses denote the number of sectors (total 55) committed to be liberalized within the ASEAN Framework of Service Agreement (AFSA).

Investment: Stages A, B, C are based on the *APEC Guidance on Investment Regime 2007*. Groups I, II, III are from *MTST Expert Team Report* (2005, Chap 4). The numbers are World Bank's EODB indexes.

Standard and Conformance: Adopted ISO, IEC, and VAP. Degree of alignment of domestic standards to international counterpart (%). *Source: MTST Expert Team Report* (2005, Chapter 5).

Customs Procedures: Harmonization with HS and WTO valuation agreement and UN/EDITFACT has already been implemented by almost all APEC economies. Scoring is based on the adoption of, or preparation for, RKC and/or the Single Window. *Sources: SCCP, CAP Accessment/Evaluation Matrix: Summary by Economy, July 2009 and SCCP, Single Window Development Report, June 2007. World Bank's Logistic Performance Index (Customs) is added in order to measure their effectiveness in individual economies.*

Intellectual Property Right: Domestic legislation of patents, designs, and trademarks and multilateral cooperation through ratifying the Paris Convention and the WTO/TRIP. In a small economy such as Brunei IPR is institutionalized in accordance with WIPO and the WTO/TRIP.

Government Procurement: Based on *MTST Expert Team Report* (2005, Chapter 9) and the most recent IAP reports. Australia and New Zealand do not participate in GPA because of their federal systems, but adopt a common GP procedure and keep transparency and competition within their bilateral FTAs. *Source: Reporting against GPEG Non-binding Principles, March 2004.*

Business Mobility: Short-term business travel and stays based on *On-line Travel Handbook* (OTH). Implementation or provisional implementation of ABTC based on the updated information by CAP, Business Visa Group.

TABLE 4.3
Five-grade Assessment by Economies and Area

	Tariffs	Services	Invest	S&C	Customs	IPR	Gov Pro	Bus Visa
Australia	5	5	5	5	5	5	4	5
Brunei	5	3	3	4	3	4	3	5
Canada	4	4	5	5	5	5	5	5
Chile	4	3	5	4	4	5	4	5
China	4	4	3	4	4	5	3	5
Hong Kong	5	3	5	4	5	4	5	5
Indonesia	4	3	3	4	3	4	4	5
Japan	4	5	5	5	5	5	5	5
South Korea	3	4	5	5	5	5	5	5
Malaysia	3	4	4	4	4	4	4	5
Mexico	3	4	4	4	3	3	3	5
New Zealand	5	4	5	5	5	5	4	5
Papua New Guinea	4	4	3	3	3	4	3	5
Peru	3	3	4	4	4	4	4	5
The Philippines	4	3	3	5	4	4	3	5
Russia	3	2	3	4	3	3	3	4
Singapore	5	4	5	5	5	5	5	5
Chinese Taipei	4	5	4	4	4	4	5	5
Thailand	3	3	4	4	4	4	4	5
United States	5	5	5	5	5	5	5	5
Vietnam	3	4	3	4	4	4	3	5
APEC Average	3.95	3.76	4.10	4.33	4.14	4.33	4.00	4.95

Figures 4.1–4.21 Radar Charts for 21 Economies

FIGURE 4.1
Australia

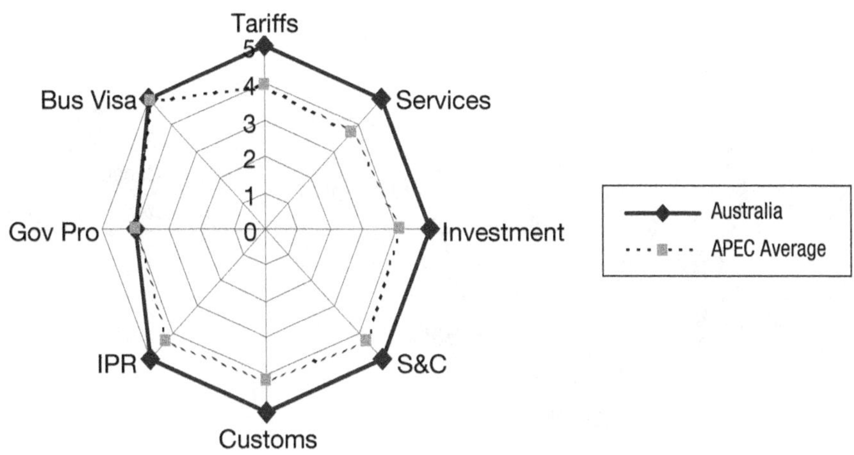

FIGURE 4.2
Brunei

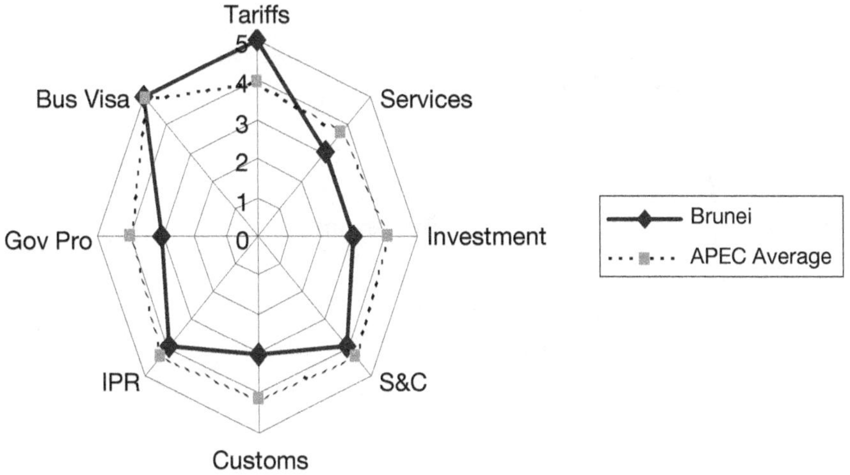

FIGURE 4.3
Canada

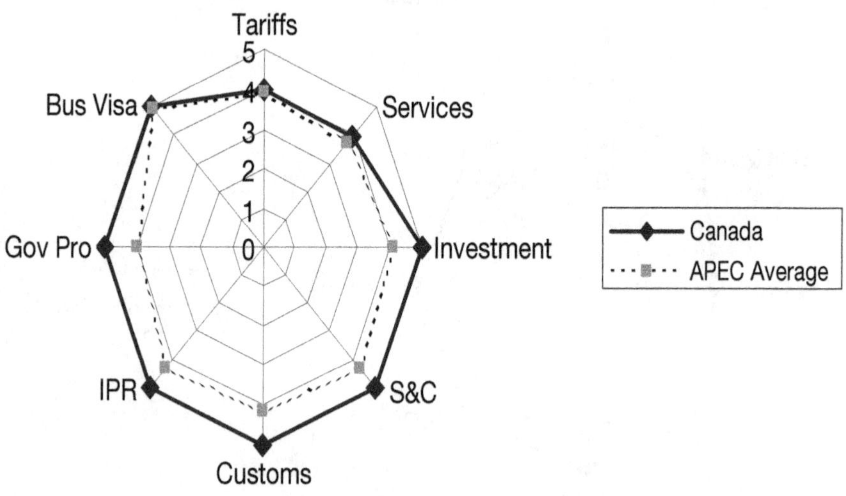

FIGURE 4.4
Chile

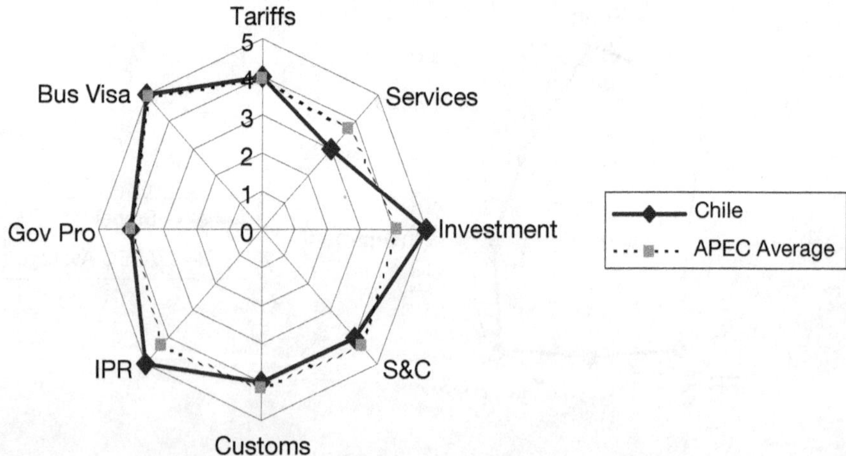

FIGURE 4.5
China

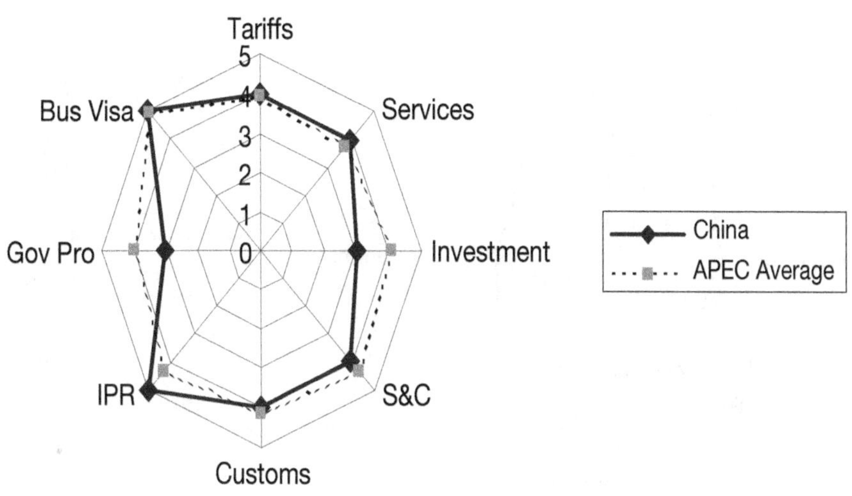

FIGURE 4.6
Hong Kong

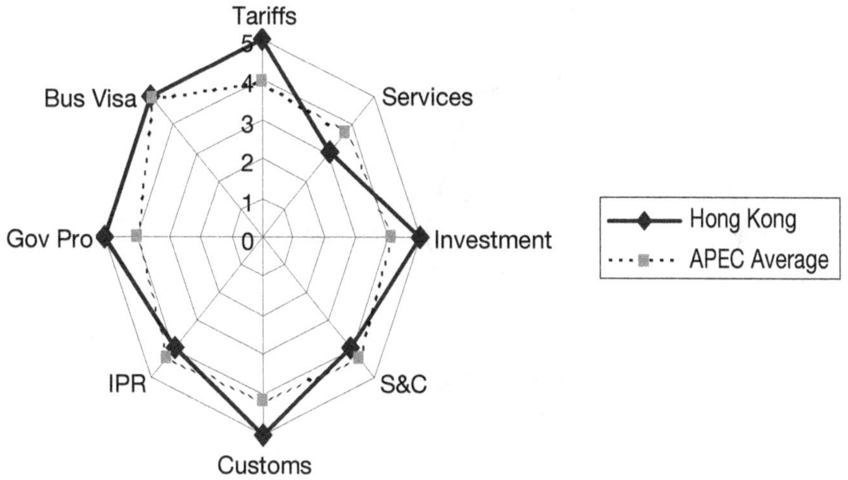

FIGURE 4.7
Indonesia

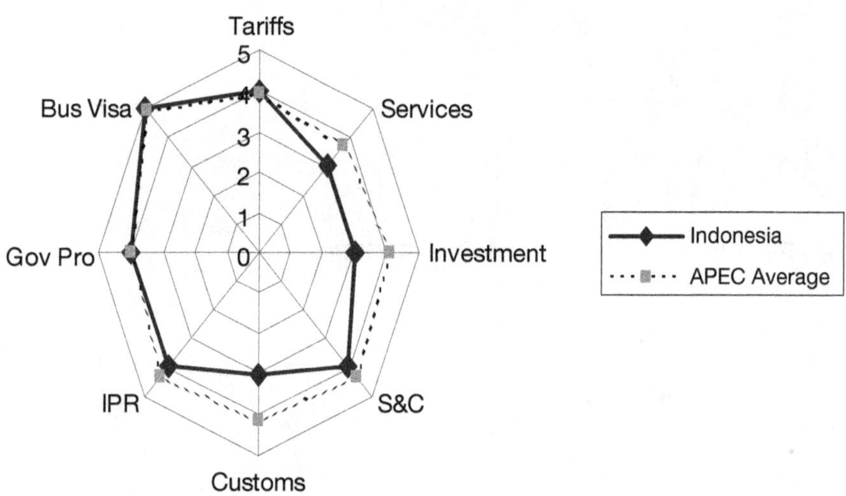

FIGURE 4.8
Japan

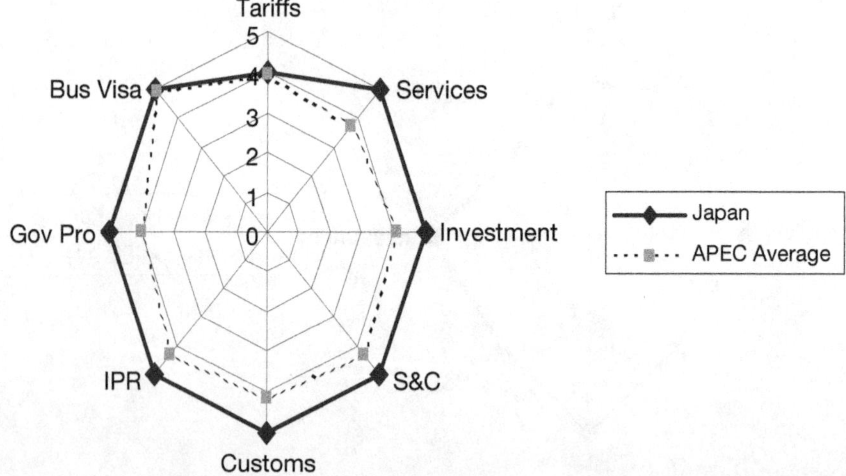

FIGURE 4.9
South Korea

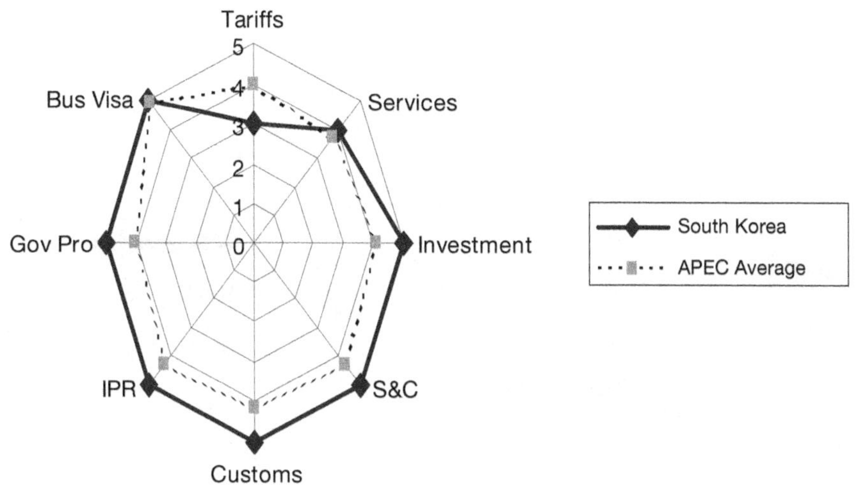

FIGURE 4.10
Malaysia

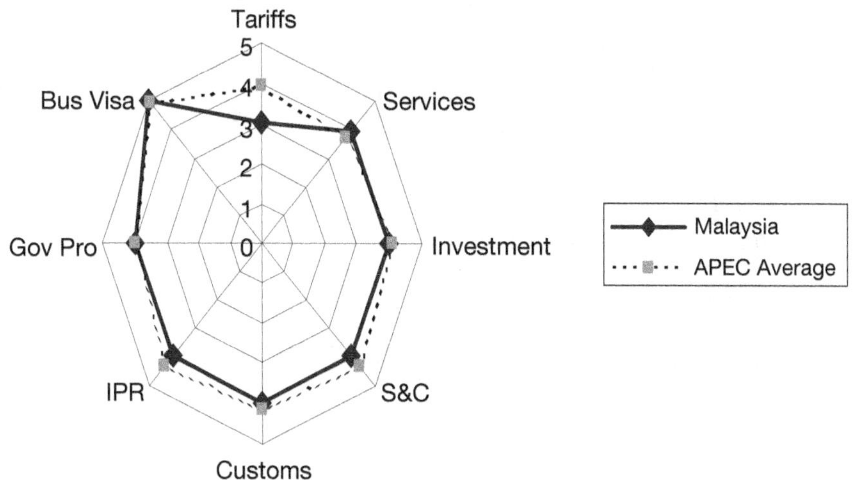

FIGURE 4.11
Mexico

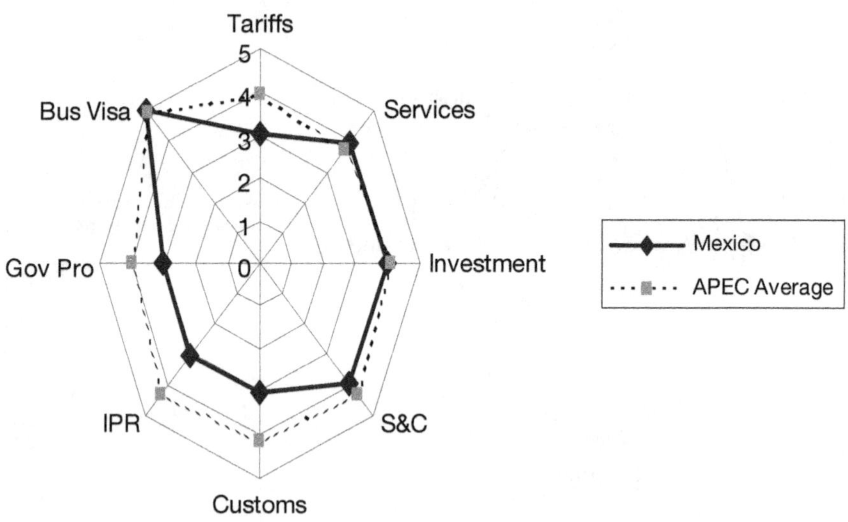

FIGURE 4.12
New Zealand

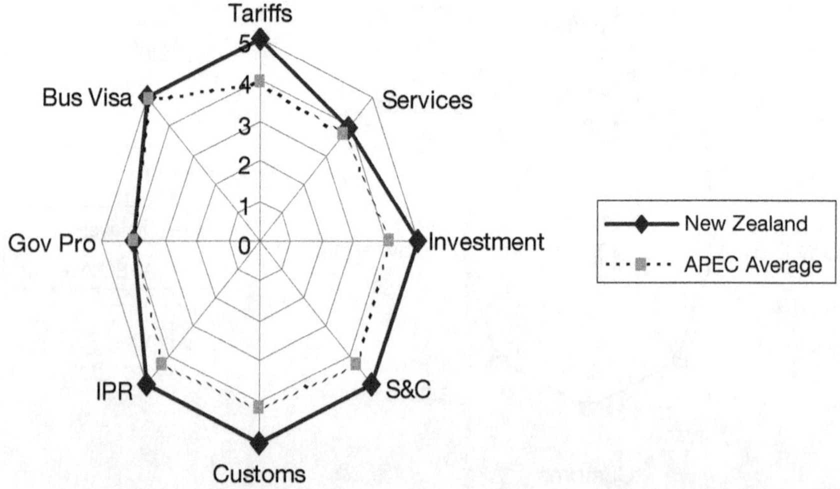

FIGURE 4.13
Peru

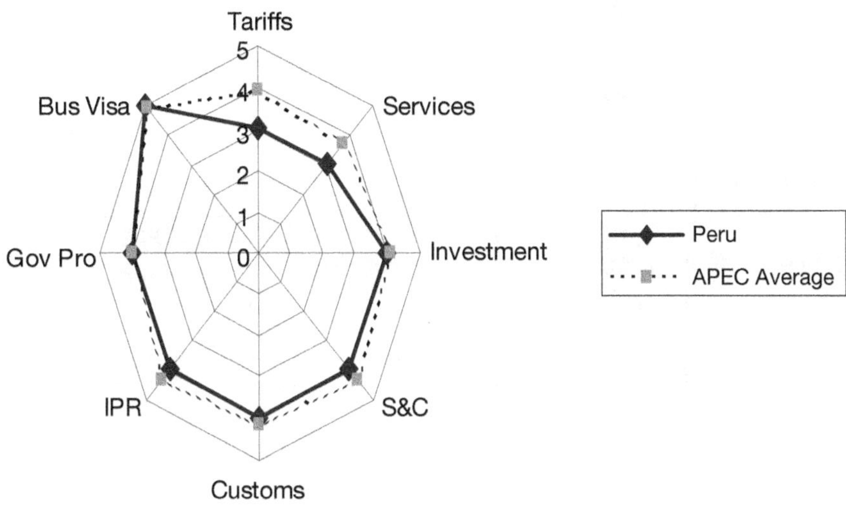

FIGURE 4.14
The Philippines

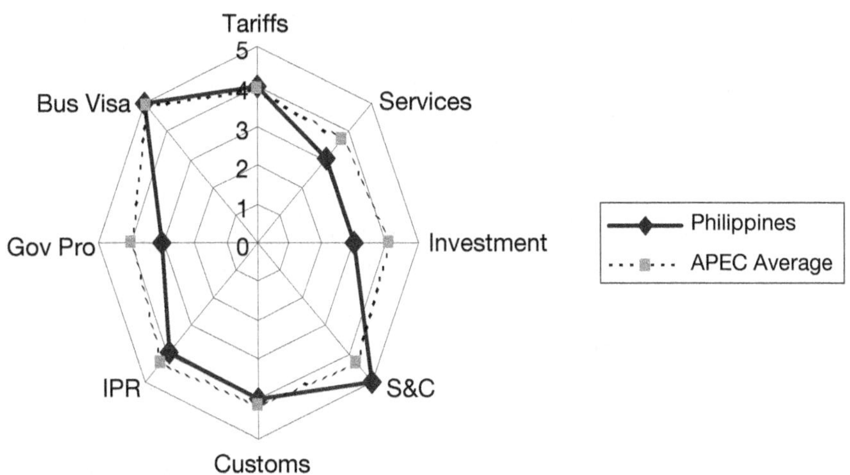

FIGURE 4.15
Papua New Guinea (PNG)

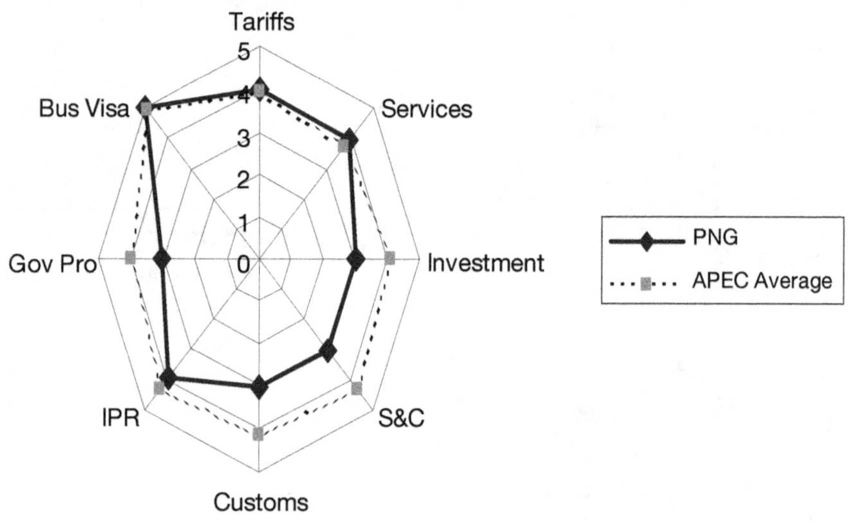

FIGURE 4.16
Russia

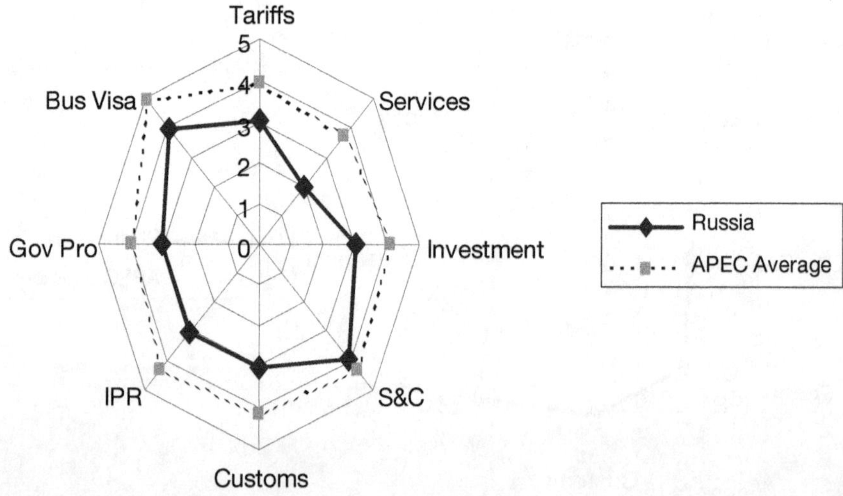

FIGURE 4.17
Singapore

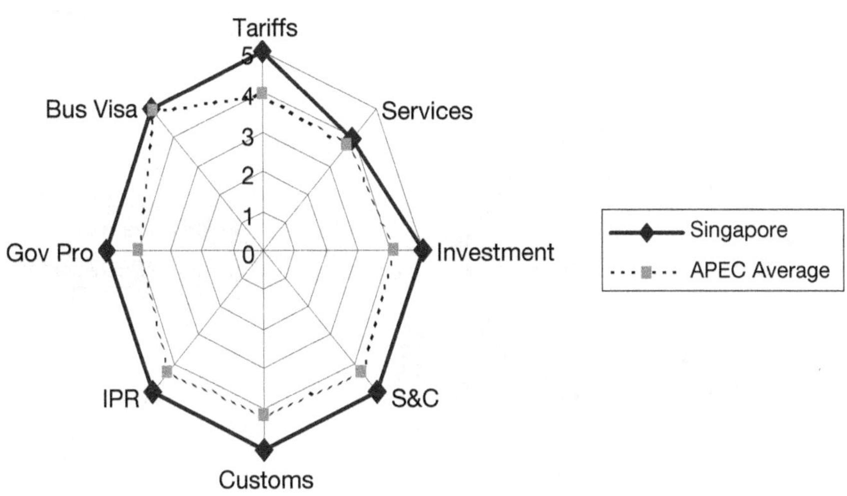

FIGURE 4.18
Chinese Taipei

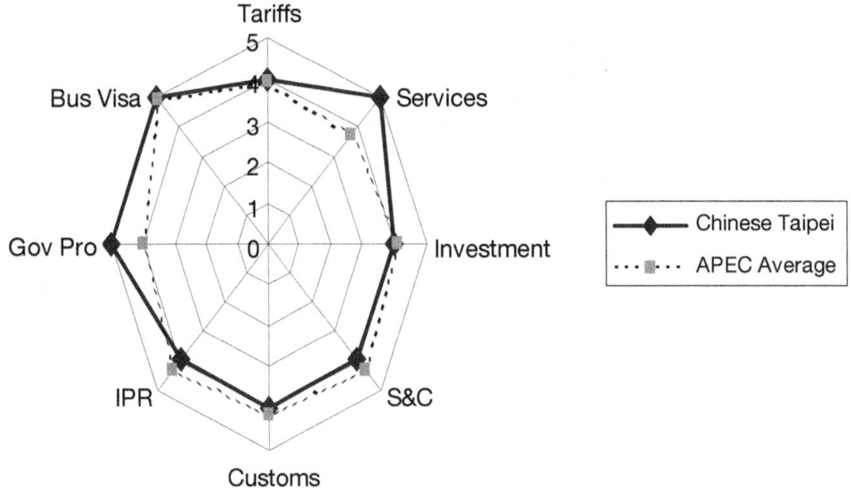

FIGURE 4.19
Thailand

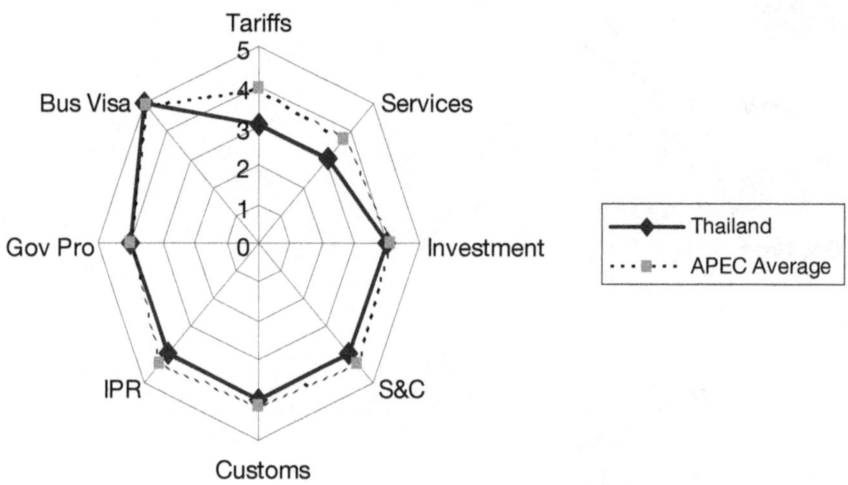

FIGURE 4.20
The United States

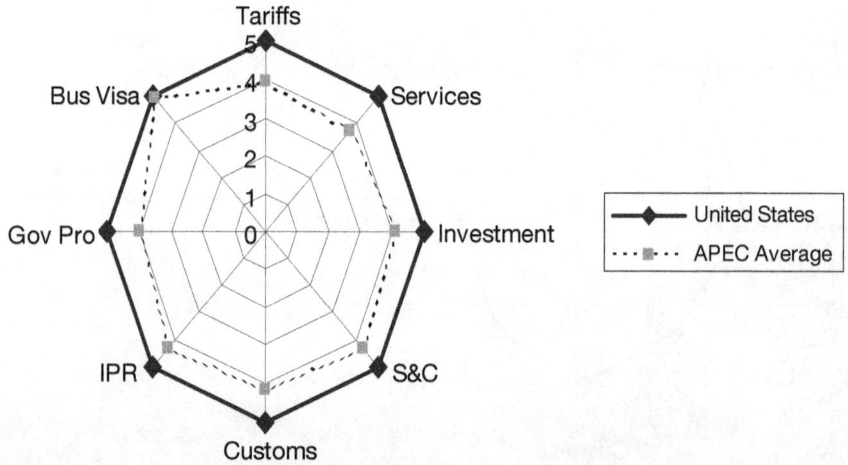

FIGURE 4.21
Vietnam

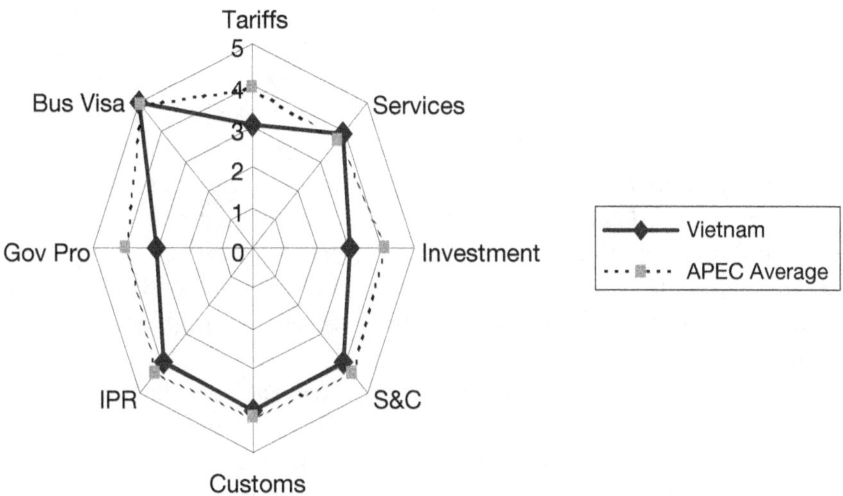

convey them in a concise way, focusing on the current levels of achievement.[3] However, the MTST expert report itself does not provide us with sufficient information for producing Table 4.2. Therefore we had to resort to supplementary data from the World Bank (Key Performance Indicators) and WTO. Only eight areas out of fifteen areas covered by the OAA are included for this reason.

Achievement by Area: Liberalization

Tariff: The OAA did not set the Bogor Goals at "zero tariffs for all commodities" but suggested the reduction of average tariffs, as well as reducing tariff peaks. APEC economies have reduced their tariffs because of the Uruguay Round Agreement (URA), but high tariffs have remained in sensitive sectors under the protracted Doha Development Agenda (DDA) negotiations. Zero tariffs have been achieved within free trade agreements (FTAs), but not on an MFN (most favoured nation) basis. Thus we set the reduction of simple average applied (SAA) MFN tariffs at less than 5 per cent as the realistic Bogor target, together with a substantial reduction of tariff peaks.

Most industrialized economies have reduced their SSA tariffs down to less than 5 per cent, but Japan and Canada still keep SSA tariffs over 5 per cent due to remaining high tariffs either on farm products or on textiles and clothing. On their part, some ASEAN (Association of Southeast Asian Nations) members and Chile have reduced their SSA tariffs down to 10 per cent or less, while keeping the WTO bound tariffs above 20–30 per cent. Australia, New Zealand, and Singapore also keep their WTO bound rates at around 10 per cent (Table 4.2). Our five grade scoring is based on the average applied rates for these economies. However, since applied rates can be raised back to the WTO bound rates at any time, it is no good to keep these high bound rates. It can only be hoped that the agricultural and non-agricultural market access negotiations be concluded in the DDA, so that remaining peak tariffs in sensitive sectors and high bound tariffs would be reduced.

Grade 5 is given to economies with SSA tariffs of 5 per cent or less, and peak tariffs proportion (of total tariff lines) of less than 5 per cent; Grade 4 to SAA tariffs of 6–10 per cent and peak tariff of less than 10 per cent; Grade 3 to SAA tariffs of 11–20 per cent and peak tariffs of less than 20 per cent; Grade 2 to SAA tariffs over 20 per cent and many tariff peaks (Table 4.1). Japan and Canada were scored 4 because their SSA tariffs have remained above 5 per cent due to high tariffs existing for agricultural products and textile and clothing.

Grade 5: Australia, Brunei, Hong Kong, New Zealand, Singapore, the United States

Grade 4: Canada, Chile, China, Indonesia, Japan, PNG, the Philippines, Chinese Taipei

Grade 3: South Korea, Malaysia, Mexico, Peru, Russia, Thailand, Vietnam[4]

Non-tariff Measures: WTO allows NTM for reasons of health, public morals, and security, and many economies have reported that they impose no NTM inconsistent with WTO rules. The OAA listed six non-tariff measures: import quotas, surcharge, minimum import price, discretionary export/import licences, voluntary export restriction, and export subsidies, and instructed each economy to enhance the transparency of its respective laws, regulations, and administrative procedures in relation to the flow of goods, services, and capital among the APEC economies and to aim towards their gradual reduction. However, the NTM summary tables, requested by the Common Format, reported the existence of NTMs in many sectors (except for New Zealand). It is hard to identify how many subsectors are subject to NTMs and how many of them are inconsistent with WTO rules.

In the meantime, the import quota on agricultural products was tarifficated under the Uruguay Round Agriculture Agreement in 2000, and bilateral quota restrictions on textiles and clothing items under the Multi-fiber Agreement were abolished by 2005.

The UNCTAD/TRAINS database used to give the frequency (proportion of total tariff lines 5224) of NTM measures for many economies and has been used for cross-country comparison. However, its comparability is now seriously impeded because of different reporting years (1994–2008), sector classification (H0, H1, H2, H3), and types of measures between APEC economies, all based on their own reporting system. Thus we have given up our quantitative assessment of NTM.

ASEAN Trade in Goods Agreement (ATIGA, concluded in 2009) is set to abolish NTMs in individual member nations in three years' time. The ASEAN Secretariat publishes detailed NTM data using the common classification, which shows high frequency ratios of NTMs of between 6 and 100 per cent, and the average of ten members of 49 per cent. APEC's peer review seems to be very lenient on NTMs.

Services: The liberalization of services trade was only included in the Uruguay Round and much less has been achieved than that for commodity trade. Various regulations are imposed on services in domestic transactions and extended to cross-border transactions. The General Agreement on Trade in Services (GATS) was concluded in the Uruguay Round in which the standard sector classification for service trade was set, and four modes of supply (cross-border supply, consumption abroad, commercial presence, and presence of natural persons), and two aspects (national treatment and market access) were identified. Individual countries report on the existence of restrictions for the individual sector, mode, and aspect, and commit not to increase restrictions (GATS Commitment Table). However, even industrialized economies keep restrictions on many service sectors, while developing economies liberalize far fewer sectors.

Reflecting the delayed liberalization in services trade in the Uruguay Round negotiations, the OAA set a much lower liberalization target for services than for commodities. It only identified four sectors — telecommunications, transportation, energy, and tourism — as priority service sectors for liberalization. Individual members' IAPs express their intention of services liberalization and list sectors to be liberalized (positive list formula). It is hard to identify from the IAPs how many sectors still remain to be liberalized.

Some progress has been made in services trade liberalization in the past fifteen years. Service trade negotiations started in 2000, ahead of the DDA, and two rounds of requests and offers were conducted by July 2008. Its final conclusion has to wait till the conclusion of the agriculture and non-agriculture market access negotiation. Some sectors are liberalized on an applied basis and expressed in the IAPs, which, however, cannot be identified easily.

The MTST Expert Team Report (2005, Chapter 3) recorded some selected economies' commitment to service liberalization that appeared in their IAPs, but these figures cannot be used for comparison. The only available data for objective assessment is GATS' Commitment Table (January 2003). We counted the number of sectors for which individual economies committed themselves to liberalize (not bound in a commitment table, fully or with limitations) either for market access and/or national treatment or both, in Mode 1 and Mode 3 of the GATS Commitment Tables 2003. Out of fifty-five sectors, industrialized economies committed to liberalizing 15–25, but developing economies committed to fewer than 15. Developing economies tend neither to commit nor be bound to many sectors that are regarded as unbound (not liberalized). Economies such as Chile, Hong Kong, and Singapore have achieved high liberalization in commodity trade, but show delays in service liberalization, while new entrants such as China and Vietnam commit to higher liberalization in services.

We give Grade 5 to economies with 9–25 liberalized sectors; Grade 4 to those with 8–15; Grade 3 to those with fewer than 6; Grade 2 to those not committed to service liberalization yet (Tables 4.1 and 4.2). These criteria may seem lenient in comparison to tariffs and investment, but takes the late start of World Trade Organization (WTO) negotiations on services liberalization into consideration. Incidentally, the European Union records 12-33-0 on an MFN basis according to the same GATS data and comes in the middle of the Grade 4 group in our criteria.

Grade 5: Australia, Japan, Chinese Taipei, the United States
Grade 4: Canada, China, South Korea, Malaysia, Mexico, New Zealand, PNG, Singapore, Vietnam, European Union

Grade 3: Brunei, Chile, Hong Kong, Indonesia, Peru, the Philippines, Thailand,
Grade 2: Russia

ASEAN has started phased liberalization in services within the ASEAN Framework Agreement on Services (AFAS 1995) since 1997 and its Commitment Table shows a much higher record (Grade 5 or 4 using our criteria) of service liberalization than on an MFN basis for economies such as Thailand, Singapore, and Indonesia (Table 4.2, Ishido 2009).

Investment: Each APEC member is eager to receive foreign investments for domestic development. As such, APEC adopted the non-binding investment principles (NBIP) as a model measure of the investment environment in 1995. Many members report in their IAPs that their own foreign investment policies and legislation are consistent with the NBIP. Most economies have set investment laws and regimes and implemented protection and redemption of profits. Many economies have joined the WTO/TRIM (trade-related investment measures) agreement and set only minimum performance requirements, then restrict FDI (foreign direct investment) or give incentives in only selected industries, and finally give national treatment to foreign investors.

The *APEC Guidebook on Investment Regimes* (2007) shows the different environments for FDI among the APEC economies. We have identified the following three stages A, B, C and scored them with Grade 5, 4, and 3 respectively.

(A) No (pre-)restriction to investments by foreign firms and gives them national treatment and MFN
(B) No regulation of foreign firms after their investment, including minimum performance requirements
(C) Protection of foreign investors against expropriation, and free redemption of profits.

The MTST Expert Team Report (2005, Chapter 4) identified three groups: Group I (transition economies), Group II (developing economies), and Group III (industrialized economies) and found that the investment environment has been improved and liberalized in the first two groups. Group III gives national treatment to foreign firms, and their screening procedure, if any, does not constrain market competition. Groups I and II either exclude particular areas (negative list) or give incentives according to their development strategy. Group I still retains many state enterprises and does not give national treatment to foreign firms. This grouping III, II, I almost corresponds to the three stages A, B, C, above respectively.

The World Bank's index for *Ease of Doing Business* (EODB) gives an objective assessment of government rule-making on business activity for 181 countries. It includes laws and regulations for both domestic and foreign businesses, and reveals the high efficiency of APEC members. Eight APEC economies are included in the top ten, together with European Union members and some oil producing countries, and seventeen APEC economies are ranked in the top half of the 181 countries. Both the MTST's grouping and the EODB index are referred to in Table 4.2, which coincides by and large with our grading above.

Grade 5: Australia, Canada, Chile, Hong Kong, Japan, South Korea, New Zealand, Singapore, the United States
Grade 4: Malaysia, Mexico, Peru, Thailand, Chinese Taipei
Grade 3: Brunei, China, Indonesia, the Philippines, PNG, Russia, Vietnam

Achievement by Area: Facilitation

In terms of the progress in facilitation areas according to the OAA (Table 4.1), the IAP/CAP (Collective Action Plan) framework worked better in the following areas due to much less domestic resistance.

Standards and Conformance (S&C): APEC issued "APEC's S&C Framework Declaration" in 1994 and established the Subcommittee for S&C (SCSC) for joint efforts in alignment to international standards and mutual recognition of conformance assessments. Individual economies' achievements, however, are constrained by their development stages. First, an economy has to build its technical infrastructure for its own standards, then participate in the International Organization for Standardization (ISO), International Electrotechnical Commission (IEC), and the Treaty of the Metre, etc. in order to align domestic standards to international ones and start mutual recognition of conformance assessment with other economies.

The Trade Facilitation Action Plan II (TFAPII 2008) reported that seventeen APEC economies have adopted the ISO, sixteen economies the IEC, seventeen economies the VAP (Voluntary Arrangement for the Pacific), and twenty economies, except Chinese Taipei, have participated in the PASC (Pacific Association for Standards and Conformance) regional forum promoting S&C. In twenty economies, except Hong Kong, industries participated in this move. Fifteen to eighteen economies participate in the MRA (Mutual Recognition Agreement) of electric and electronics, food and labour accreditation. Brunei has adopted international standards instead of setting its own standards. Thus all APEC economies are eager to have international alignment and are closer to achieving the Bogor Goals.

Grade 5 is given to economies that have achieved a high level of international alignment and expanding MRA; Grade 4 to those with ISO and IEC, but starting MRA; Grade 3 to those that have achieved only half of international alignment; Grade 2 to those only now setting domestic standards and preparing administrative agencies (Tables 4.1 and 4.2).

Grade 5: Australia, Canada, Japan, South Korea, New Zealand, the Philippines, Singapore, the United States

Grade 4: Brunei, Chile, China, Hong Kong, Indonesia, Malaysia, Mexico, Peru, Russia, Chinese Taipei, Thailand, Vietnam

Grade 3: PNG

Customs Procedures: The Subcommittee on Custom Procedures (SCCP) has made great progress in modernizing customs administration in APEC member governments over the past years. This has included substantial improvement in promptness, transparency, and predictability in customs procedures, and an improved trade and investment environment for businesses across the region. Its impact is multiplied when it is implemented jointly by as many economies as possible. The OAA has set concrete objectives for collective action such as the harmonization of tariff structures with the Harmonized System Convention (HSC), adoption of the principles of the WTO valuation agreement, simplification and harmonization on the basis of the Kyoto Convention, transparency of customs procedures, customs laws, regulations, administrative guidelines, procedures, and rulings, and adoption of the UN/EDIFACT (Electronic Data Interchange for Administration, Commerce and Transport), etc. Most members have adopted the first two objectives. The UN/EDIFACT is implemented by many members and the average length of time required for customs clearance has been significantly shortened.

The revised Kyoto Convention has been in force since February 2006 and nine economies have adopted it, while six economies are now in preparation for it. The Single Window has been introduced since 2006 so traders complete customs clearance and documentation together with quarantine at the first entry point. Capacity building required for facilitating this programme was provided by technical assistance organized by CAP. Single Window has been introduced by five economies, while fourteen other economies are now preparing for it. Furthermore, the WCO framework has been implemented by twelve economies in order to secure international trade against terrorism. Both the Single Window and WCO were invented after the Bogor Declaration, but spread and were implemented much earlier than in other regions, thanks to the APEC process.

Grade 5 is given to the economies which adopted the revised Kyoto Convention and introduced the Single Window; Grade 4 to those preparing for the revised Kyoto Convention and the Single Window; Grade 3 to those that have adopted HSC, Valuation Agreement, and UN/EDIFACT; Grade 2 to those still preparing their customs procedures.

The World Bank's Logistic Performance Index (LPI; Customs) measures the effectiveness of these institutional arrangements. Fourteen APEC economies are ranked within the top quarter of 150 economies, together with seventeen European Union members. It should be noted that APEC has achieved as high a level of simplified and standardized customs procedures as the European Union with a single piece of legislation and well-established enforcement mechanism. LPI is also referred to in the scoring above (Tables 4.1 and 4.2).

Grade 5: Australia, Canada, Hong Kong, Japan, South Korea, New Zealand, Singapore, the United States
Grade 4: Chile, China, Malaysia, Peru, the Philippines, Chinese Taipei, Thailand, Vietnam
Grade 3: Brunei, Indonesia, Mexico, PNG, Russia

Intellectual Property Rights (IPR): The protection of IPR is a prerequisite for technology and know-how to be transferred smoothly and better utilized across borders. The OAA sets objectives to ensure the adequate and effective protection of IPR, including legislation, administration, and enforcement in the Asia Pacific region based on the principles of MFN treatment, national treatment, and transparency, as set out in the WTO/TRIPS (Trade-Related Aspects of Intellectual Property Rights) agreement (1994) and other related agreements. This has been well perceived by all APEC members and most members ratified TRIPS and the Paris Convention for industrial patents.

All economies have adopted a patent law, design law, and trade marks. The Paris Convention, the multilateral framework for protecting

IPR in industry, has been ratified by eighteen APEC economies except Brunei, Russia, and Chinese Taipei. WTO/TRIPS has been ratified by nineteen APEC economies except Brunei and Russia. Grade 5 is given to the economies that have adopted the Paris Convention and WTO/TRIPS; Grade 4 to those with effective enforcement of IPR; Grade 3 to those that have adopted domestic legislation of patents, designs, and trade marks; Grade 2 to those preparing for IPR protection and enforcement.

Grade 5: Australia, Canada, Chile, China, Japan, South Korea, New Zealand, Singapore, the United States
Grade 4: Brunei, Hong Kong, Indonesia, Malaysia, Peru, the Philippines, PNG, Chinese Taipei, Thailand, Vietnam
Grade 3: Mexico, Russia

However, the effectiveness of the implementation of IPR cannot be assessed from the IAP and MTST reports. IPR is still a major cause of trade and investment disputes and its implementation needs to be improved through consultation and negotiation.

Government Procurement: As regards government procurement, the priority purchase of domestic products has long been acknowledged as the reason for national security and industry protection (exempted from national treatment in GATT Article 3). However, because of the globalization of businesses, government procurement transactions have necessitated the demand for an open and competitive market for government procurements. The Government Procurement Agreement (GPA) was ratified as a part of the Marrakech Treaty in 1994, which covers both commodities and services, and includes local governments and other public organizations as well. However, the decentralization of government administration differs among APEC members, and because of this the OAA did not emphasize the liberalization of government procurement, but insisted on the transparency of legislature and procedures and its international dissemination. In 1995 APEC adopted a model measure, the "Government Procurement Non-Binding Principles of Transparency, Value for Money, Open and Effective Competition, Fair Dealing, Accountability and Due Process, and Non-discrimination" and encouraged individual members to align their own procedures to this. Six APEC economies have ratified GPA and China is preparing to do so.

Grade 5 is given to the economies which have already ratified WTO/GPA; Grade 4 to those that have implemented e-bidding and related facilities; Grade 3 to those that have arranged government procurement procedures and its transparency; Grade 2 to those in the preparatory stage.

In the current global financial crisis, economies such as the United States, Indonesia, and major states of Australia have applied to buy home-produced products and services for government procurements. The United States, as a signatory country of the GPA, exempted other GPA signatories from this Buy-American policy, while Australia and Indonesia, non-signatory countries, can discriminate against other APEC economies under these measures.

Grade 5: Canada, Hong Kong, Japan, South Korea, Singapore, Chinese Taipei, the United States
Grade 4: Australia, Chile, Indonesia, Malaysia, New Zealand, Peru, Thailand
Grade 3: Brunei, China, Mexico, the Philippines, PNG, Russia, Vietnam

Business Mobility: The OAA adopted the enhancement of the mobility of business people as a strategic approach to facilitate trade and investment expansion in the region, in response to a strong request by ABAC (APEC Business Advisory Council). The Group of Business Mobility started in 1997 and focused on transparent legislation for the business visa and short-term business stay. It also suggested that individual economies publish the *APEC Business Travel Handbook (ABTH)* and issued the APEC Business Travel Card (ABTC). The handbook collects and disseminates information on the processing of visas, application procedures, and the terms of validity. The Travel Card provides privileged lanes for guaranteed business travellers at immigration offices.

All APEC economies have already published the *ABTH*. The ABTC was started by a few proponent economies and was followed up by eight economies by 2000, but had not spread further due to political and security reasons (Feinberg and Zhan 2001). Some members have also strengthened immigration procedures to counter terrorism since 2001. However, it has now been adopted by twenty APEC economies except for Russia. Grade 5 is given to twenty economies for fulfilling both *ABTH* and ABTC, and Grade 4 to Russia for having published the *ABTH* but not having implemented the ABTC yet.

Canada and the United States require a visa under the provisional implementation of ABTC, but privileged lanes are available. Both economies have strengthened their entry procedures. For short-term stays not exceeding 90 days in the United States, travellers of six APEC economies can use the ESTA (Electronic System for Travel Authorization) programme without a visa. Incidentally, the issue of ABTCs increased by between 50 to 75 per cent annually for the period 2006–09, with its accumulated total amounting to 69,000 by the end of June 2009.[5] With both *ABTH* and ABTC fulfilled by most economies, APEC has almost completely achieved its goal in this area.

Grade 5: All economies except for Russia
Grade 4: Russia

Nevertheless, some argue for the need to ease the mobility of semi-skilled and unskilled workers across borders. It is a desirable direction for APEC to pursue in the long run, but it is certainly beyond the Bogor Goals. Incidentally ASEAN has started to liberalize the movement of skilled workers (engineers, nurses, accountants, and medical doctors) among members in its ASEAN Economic Community Blueprint (2008).

Other Areas: The preceding assessment still leaves five areas of the OAA — Competition Policy, Deregulation, Rules of Origin (ROO), Dispute Settlement, and Implementation of the URA (Table 4.1) — to be evaluated. As competition policy and deregulation have only been broadly stated in the OAA, and there is no consensus on the specific goals or scope of competition policy or deregulation among members as they are at different stages of industrialization and operate under different institutional and legal structures, APEC members have not been able to report their IAPs in a standardized manner. They were stressed again as "behind-the-border measures" and reset as a Structural Reform programme under the Economic Committee in 2005 (Chapter 5).

The ROO goal originally aimed at collecting information about different ROOs in the preferential and non-preferential ROOs among APEC members, and promoting their harmonization. As the DDA negotiation has been protracted and unresolved, and bilateral and regional FTAs have been flourishing worldwide, ROOs have become the focus of APEC's Model Measures for FTAs (Chapter 5). Dispute settlement is still an important task for APEC members. However, many members have tended to resort to the WTO panels for dispute settlement and the "APEC Dispute Mediation System" proposed by the EPG (Eminent Persons Group)

Report III has not been developed so far (APEC 1995). Meanwhile the implementation of the URA has been completed. The first three areas have been worked into the new APEC agenda, but it is too early to assess the extent to which they have been achieved.

Overall Assessment of the Mid-term Bogor Goals

Table 4.3 provides a summary matrix of scores of twenty-one economies by eight areas. The last row gives the average scores, or average achievement, of the twenty-one economies in individual areas. Business mobility has achieved the highest score, 4.95, which means the Bogor Goal for this is almost complete. It is followed by Standards and Conformance and Intellectual Property Rights, both at 4.33, by Customs Procedures at 4.14, and Government Procurement at 4.00. All facilitation areas achieved a score of 4 or more, that is, "completed with important exceptions". In the liberalization areas, the APEC average scores are lower; 4.10 in Investment, 3.95 in Tariffs, and 3.76 in Services. Are they not far from the perception of many observers about APEC's achievements by areas? It should be noted that half of APEC economies have achieved an integrated market in investment and customs procedures, comparable with European Union members, while APEC is far behind the European Union in institutional integration.

We do not calculate the total scores of individual economies in all areas. It is because we do not aim to rank them by their total scores, but to examine individual economies' patterns of achievement by areas. It is shown in the radar charts in Figures 4.1–4.21, which measure each economy's scores of 1 to 5 from the centre along the eight axes. The solid line gives the economy's scores, while the dotted line gives the APEC average. The outermost line linking 5 along all axes reflects the highest achievement, that is, the complete achievement of the Bogor Goals. The radar chart shows concisely the pattern of the degree of achievement of each individual economy of the Bogor Goals.

The following three patterns are identified.

(A) Economies that have achieved 5 in most areas, but 4 in one or two areas: Australia, Canada, Japan, New Zealand, Singapore, and Hong Kong have this pattern, while the United States has achieved 5 in all areas.

(B) Economies duplicating the APEC average line in many areas: China, Malaysia, Peru, the Philippines, and Thailand belong to this pattern.
(C) Economies enclosed within the APEC average line: PNG, Russia, and Vietnam belong to this pattern.

Chile, South Korea, and Chinese Taipei come in between (A) and (B), and Indonesia, Mexico, and Brunei Darussalam come in between (B) and (C).

Figures 4.1–4.21 show us the extent of APEC economies' progress towards the Bogor Goals. Here it should be noted that these reflect the current level of their achievements, but do not measure the accumulated efforts of individual economies in liberalization and facilitation for the past fifteen years. As I repeatedly said in my assessment of achievements in individual areas in the preceding two sections, the institutional achievement in liberalization and facilitation have been constrained by each economy's stage of economic development and experience in market economies. As the MTST Expert Team Report (2005) pointed out, the progress in liberalization in investment was greater in developing economies and transition economies. Industrialized economies had already achieved high levels of liberalization at the time of the Bogor Declaration, and it is quite natural for them to have acquired higher scores in this assessment work.

APEC 2010 and Beyond

APEC SOM reported the mid-term assessment of the progress towards the Bogor Goals to the Leaders' Meeting in 2010. The goals included five industrialized economies designated to achieve free and open trade by 2010, plus eight economies which volunteered to assessment this time, namely Chile, Hong Kong, South Korea, Malaysia, Mexico, Peru, Singapore, and Chinese Taipei. They were not assessed individually, but as a group of five plus eight economies.

APEC/LM (2010*b*) summarized the achievements of the thirteen economies as follows: Overall growth in commodity trade for all APEC economies increased by 7.1 per cent annually from 1994 to 2009, services by 7 per cent, and inflow and outflow of FDI by 13 per cent and 12.7 per cent respectively. The thirteen economies reduced their simple average tariffs from 8.2 per cent to 5.4 per cent for 1994–2009, far lower than the world average of 10.4 per cent, as well as further tariff reduction within their FTA framework. They opened their services markets through unilateral reform of domestic policy and maintained liberalized investment regimes. They also took significant steps towards trade facilitation to streamline customs procedures and align standards and conformance procedures. Under the Trade Facilitation Action Plan (TFAP) they reduced transaction costs in the region by 5 per cent for the period 2002–06 and are achieving an additional 5 per cent under the second TFAP this year.

On the other hand, APEC/LM (2010*b*) also noted that impediments still remain in sensitive sectors:

- higher tariffs remain for agricultural products and textiles and clothing
- restrictions remain in financial, telecommunications, transportation, and audiovisual services, and the movement of people is least liberalized
- sectoral investment restrictions exist in the form of prohibitions or capital ceiling and continuing general screening systems
- Further efforts are needed for non-tariff measures
- Further work needs to be done for standards and conformance, customs procedures, intellectual property rights, and government procurement
- Behind-the-border issues need to be addressed by facilitating structural reform

The Leaders concluded with the following statements:

> It is a fair statement to say that the 2010 economies have some way to go to achieve free and open trade in the region. APEC challenges in pursuing free and open trade and investment continues. APEC will continue to review economies' progress towards the Bogor Goals of free and open trade and investment. We recognized that all APEC economies must maintain their individual and collective commitment to further liberalize and facilitate trade and investment by reducing or eliminating tariffs, restrictions on trade in services, and restrictions on investment, and promoting improvement in other areas, including non-tariff measures and behind-the-border issues.
>
> ...APEC has achieved much since its inception, evolving to become the pre-eminent economic forum in the Asia-Pacific, the world's most dynamic and open region. Looking back over the past 15 years, the progress made by APEC in pursuit of the goal of free and open trade and investment has

> reinforced the fact that full achievement of the Bogor Goals for all economies should continue to provide direction for APEC's work of trade and investment liberalization and facilitation. (APEC/LM 2010b)

This is a fair assessment of APEC's achievement, considering the severe constraints that hobbled the WTO/DDA negotiation, and the Bogor process has been implemented under the modality of non-binding liberalization. APEC's TILF process will continue for all APEC economies, including the thirteen economies noted here. However, it is not clear from the leaders' statements and report how this process will be conducted. Will all twenty-one economies conduct the peer review process of IAP/CAP at SOM? Will the thirteen economies assessed this time be given a new form of review, focusing on their remaining impediments? Will all twenty-one economies be subject to a new review process towards the final target of 2020?

SOM1 and 2 in 2011 will clarify these in due course, but we wish to see the TILF process continued towards further achievement of the Bogor Goals as the leaders committed in their declaration. The past three rounds of the IAP review process have been criticized because of its huge scope and ambiguous focus due to its positive list formula. How many readers did it gain every year? This is a good opportunity to reasses the IAP review process towards the 2020 goal.

Throughout 2010 APEC senior officials undertook a detailed examination of individual economies' achievements in individual TILF areas, including self assessment by the thirteen volunteer economies, the assessment report by the Policy Support Unit, the three rounds of IAP peer reviews for the past decade, and mid-term stock-takes in 2005, to produce a SOM report (APEC/SOM 2010) at SOM1 to 3. While the final report tells us only the group assessment of the thirteen volunteer economies, individual senior officials, from both the thirteen economies and the rest of APEC, have understood well how far they have progressed towards the Bogor Goals and how much still remains to do. The six sectors listed in the leaders' assessment (APEC/SOM 2010*b*) cited above suggest the direction for their further efforts. Their findings should be fully utilized for the second half of the Bogor process.

This chapter gives an independent quantitative assessment that the thirteen economies differed greatly in their progress and that the remaining eight economies have achieved much less towards the Bogor Goals. They may be treated differently according to their different extent of liberalization and facilitation. Which areas do the thirteen economies list as those they perceive as making insufficient progress to be able to achieve the Boger Goals? The list of six sectors cited from the leaders' assessment provides a common IAP negative list reporting format. However, it is no use for the remaining eight economies to continue their current IAP reporting format. They may be better advised to change it to the IAP negative list formula to be submitted every three years. It will make the IAP process more effective in promoting liberalization and facilitation on a non-binding basis in a more concerted way, which will pave the road towards a FTAAP (Free Trade Area of the Asia Pacific).[6]

Notes

1. In December 2009 Japanese senior officials organized an "APEC Japan 2010 Symposium" in Tokyo in order to invite advice from senior officials and experts about the possible agenda for APEC 2010. The author was invited to give his quantitative assessment of the progress towards the Bogor Goals by the twenty-one individual economies, in the first draft of this chapter.
2. The Policy Support Unit of the APEC Secretariat submitted its assessment of the progress towards the Bogor Goals by "5 industrialized economies plus 4 economies volunteered to be assessed", which only gives group assessments of five and five plus four.
3. The present author conducted a quantitative assessment of APEC's liberalization and facilitation in 1997 (Yamazawa and Urata 2000), which was based more on future commitments, while the present assessment examined the current achievements.
4. An expert commented on my five grade scoring missing "grade 1 or 2" in some areas. However, my grading is not a relative grading in which all economies are classified into 10-20-40-20-10 per cent for 1–5, but absolute grading listed in Table 4.1. Since they have implemented IAPs for fifteen years after the Bogor Declaration, it is natural that few economies remain at Grade 2 or 1 in many areas.
5. Readers may think that the two measures in Business Mobility are easy to accomplish. However, in the early 2000s, only several economies had implemented the two, so that a reviewer was pessimistic about their future prospect (Feinberg and Zhao 2001).
6. A new IAP peer review process was agreed at SOM2 in late May 2011. All 21 economies will continue to submit an AIP every other year in a refined format towards 2020.

5

Realistic Approach over the Past Decade

The Busan Road Map: Towards a Better Business Environment

In Chapter 2 we saw that APEC's momentum for liberalization heightened in 1993–96, but decreased after the Asian currency crisis. Instead APEC has shifted to a realistic strategy of improving the business environment of its participants in the first decade of the twenty-first century. Although APEC is strictly constrained in its liberalization attempts by its non-binding framework, many economies have voluntarily implemented facilitation measures such as standards and conformance, customs procedures, and business mobility once they find that it helps their own trade and investment expansion. With increasing globalization and people, goods, and money moving freely across borders in the 2000s, these facilitation measures made a big contribution towards this development. As was shown in Chapter 2, the ratio of commodity trade, services, and direct investment to GDP increased distinctly in many economies. This ratio differs according to the size of an economy, but in the 2000s it increased in all economies, regardless of their size. The increase was most distinct in the European Union, but APEC economies followed the European Union closely (Chapter 2). Let us pick up major measures highlighted in the various Leaders' and Ministerial Statements.

In 2000, in Bandar Seri Begawan, Brunei, the APEC leaders committed to not letting any economy be left behind the digital divide under the IT revolution. The following year in Shanghai, they announced the Shanghai Accord of "reducing the business transaction cost across border by 5% for five years". In 2002, at the APEC Conference in Mexico, the Trade Facilitation Action Plan (TFAP I: 2002–06) was established and promptly implemented. It instructed the abolition of administrative barriers in standards and conformance, customs procedures, and business mobility. It duplicated the Osaka Action Agenda towards achieving the Bogor Goals, but strengthened it by setting a concrete target of "reducing 5% in 5 years". This tended to be offset by the prolonged customs procedures put in place under strengthened security systems at airports and harbours after the 11 September attacks in 2001, but they managed to achieve this target.

In 2004, in Santiago, Chile, APEC leaders took up the issue of reduction of public and private corruption, and announced the Santiago Commitment on APEC actions for anti-corruption and transparency. In 2005 the APEC Conference in Busan established the second Trade Facilitation Action Plan (TFAP II: 2006–10), which committed to the further reduction of transaction costs by 5 per cent for five years. The newly established Policy Support Unit is now checking its achievement. I gave high grades to many APEC economies for these three facilitation areas in Chapter 4, which apparently owed much to TFAP I and II.

In Busan APEC also announced the Busan Road Map including the TFAP II. It contained the Mid-Term Stock-take (MTST) of IAP/CAP efforts towards the achievement of the Bogor Goals as well as the Busan Business Agenda. The latter listed measures for improving the business environment in response to a strong request by ABAC (APEC Business Advisory Council), which included assistance for capacity building to middle- and small-sized firms, counterfeit and pirate practices, and "Secure Trade in APEC Regions" (STAR).

In 2006 the APEC conference in Hanoi set up the Hanoi Action Plan for implementing the Busan Road Map. It detailed an annual schedule of policy measures designated by the Busan Road Map, apparently in the expectation that these measures would be reflected in the IAP/CAPs (Individual Action Plan/Collective Action Plans) of individual economies.[1]

APEC Programmes for Strengthening Regional Integration

Another distinct phenomenon in the international economic environment in the 2000s is the worldwide spread of FTAs (free trade agreements). East Asia, while following this trend, lags behind other regions, but bilateral FTAs mushroomed both among APEC economies and with outside partners. ASEAN (Association of Southeast Asian Nations) took the lead in this trend. It accelerated the completion of an ASEAN Free Trade Area (AFTA) by two years, and moved to a deeper market integration towards an economic community. It also concluded "ASEAN+1" type of FTAs with China, South Korea, Japan, and Australia/New Zealand (Fig. 5.1). APEC had so far pursued unilateral liberalization and supported the WTO/ DDA (World Trade Organization/Doha Development Agenda) negotiation. However, while the DDA negotiation has stumbled due to the conflict of

TABLE 5.1
Trade Agreements in the APEC Region

1983:	Australia-New Zealand Closer Economic Relations Agreement (ANZCERTA)
1989:	U.S.-Canada Free Trade Agreement (USCFTA)
1992:	ASEAN Free Trade Agreement (AFTA)
1994:	North America Free Trade Agreement (NAFTA)
1997:	Canada-Chile Free Trade Agreement
1999:	Chile-Mexico Free Trade Agreement
2001:	New Zealand–Singapore Free Trade Agreement
2002:	Japan-Singapore Economic Partnership Agreement (EPA)
2003:	Australia-Singapore Free Trade Agreement ASEAN-China FTA (trade in goods)
2004:	Chile-Korea FTA, China–Hong Kong FTA, U.S.-Chile FTA, Singapore-USA FTA
2005:	Australia-USA FTA, Japan-Mexico EPA, New Zealand–Thailand FTA, Australia-Thailand FTA
2006:	Chile-China FTA, Japan-Malaysia EPA, Korea-Singapore FTA, Trans-Pacific Strategic Partnership Agreement (P4)
2007:	Chile-Japan EPA, Japan-Thailand EPA, ASEAN-China FTA (services)
2008:	Brunei-Japan EPA, Indonesia-Japan EPA, New Zealand–China FTA, ASEAN-Korea Framework Agreement, U.S.-Korea FTA (not ratified yet)
2010:	Australia-Chile FTA, Canada-Peru FTA, China-Singapore FTA, Japan-Philippines EPA, Peru-Singapore FTA. Peru-U.S. FTA (not ratified yet), ASEAN-Japan Comprehensive Economic Partnership Agreement (CEP), ASEAN-Australia, New Zealand FTA

interests of major participants, APEC obviously has not shied away from FTAs within itself.

PECC (Pacific Economic Cooperation Council) experts and ABAC then began to express their concern about the spread of FTAs, a concern apparently originating from non-Asians' anxiety about being discriminated against by the spread of bilateral and plural FTAs in East Asia. They criticized the "spaghetti-bowl effect" — often rephrased as "noodle-bowl effect" in East Asia — in which divergent contents of these FTAs tend to obstruct business across borders.

Japan was one of the initiators of FTAs in East Asia. It changed its traditional stance of supporting only multilateral negotiations and started a preparatory study of the Japan-Korea FTA in 1999. In 2002 it concluded the Japan-Singapore EPA (Economic Partnership Agreement), which turned out to be a new type of agreement that includes services and related behind-the-border measures and which responds better to current business needs than a conventional FTA covering only commodity trade.[2] Thereafter Japan negotiated a bilateral EPA with Mexico, Malaysia, Indonesia, the Philippines, Thailand, and Vietnam as well as the ASEAN-Japan Comprehensive Economic Partnership (CEP) agreement. PECC's concern about FTAs partly stemmed from this change in Japan's commercial strategy. On my part, I supported this strategy change on the grounds that it would help Japan to get rid of the decade-long recession of the 1990s. Instead of being left behind the global trend of FTAs, an active commercial policy would spur dynamism in her domestic economy.[3] I argued this point against PECC experts and suggested that East Asia was a latecomer in this worldwide tendency and no serious "spaghetti-bowl" effect was witnessed in East Asia.[4]

Other East Asian economies — including Singapore, Thailand, China, and South Korea — have begun negotiating bilateral or plural FTAs either within or outside APEC, and the China-ASEAN FTA and Korea-ASEAN FTA, both covering only commodity trade, were concluded before the Japan-ASEAN CEP. Outside East Asia, Chile and New Zealand have concluded many FTAs within and outside APEC, and have become a hub of FTAs respectively. Australia concluded FTAs with Thailand and the United States besides the closer Economic Relationship (CER) agreement with neighbour New Zealand. A positive assessment of FTAs has emerged from APEC, which aims at utilizing them for APEC liberalization.

If FTAs concluded between different pairs or groups are harmonized using the liberalization formula, rules of origin, coverage of transaction, and other components, the spaghetti-bowl effect will be minimized so it will be easier to forge linkages among themselves, towards greater liberalization within APEC.[5] In 2004 PECC drafted "The APEC Best Practices for RTAs/FTAs" and APEC/MM (Ministerial Meeting) adopted it at the suggestion of ABAC (PECC 2004). In 2005 in Busan, APEC leaders declared that APEC economies should conclude as many RTAs (Regional Trade Agreements)/FTAs as possible, so as to promote liberalization in APEC (APEC/LM 2005). APEC/MM instructed SOM to produce a detailed set of best practice RTAs/FTAs (APEC/MM 2005).

In 2006, the APEC conference in Hanoi instructed a study of how APEC should deal with the spread of RTAs/FTAs and a SOM's report, "The APEC Initiative for Strengthening Regional Integration", was submitted at the APEC conference in Sydney in 2007. The report reviewed the process of deepening regional economic integration in the APEC region, focusing on TILF (trade and investment liberalization and facilitation), and searched for the future direction of APEC. It endorsed further efforts towards achieving the Bogor Goals and expected that it would also lay the foundation for "a possible Free Trade Area of the Asia-Pacific (FTAAP) in the long term".

SOM continued its work and published APEC's Agenda for Regional Economic Integration, detailing concrete actions as follow (APEC 2008):

- Strong support from APEC economies to bring the Doha Round to a successful conclusion in 2008
- Compilation of a preliminary inventory of issues relevant to an FTAAP
- Completion of the initial tranche of a study on identifying convergences and divergences in APEC RTAs/FTAs
- Exploration of the concepts of enlargement, docking, or merging of existing agreements
- Completion of APEC model measures for RTAs and FTAs
- Endorsement of key performance indicators for TFAP II
- Establishment of the APEC Investment Facilitation Action Plan (IFAP) endorsed by trade ministers
- Successful establishment of APEC Policy Support Unit

FTAAP will be discussed in the next chapter. Issues related to TFAP and IFAP are now in progress. Let me review the APEC model measures for RTAs/FTAs here.

TABLE 5.2
APEC's Model Measures for RTAs/FTAs

Chapeau
Safeguards
Competition Policy
Environment
Temporary Entry for Business Persons
Customs Administration and Trade Facilitation
Electronic Commerce
Rules of Origin and Origin Procedures
Sanitary and Phyto-sanitary measures
Trade in Goods
Technical Barriers to Trade
Transparency
Government Procurement
Cooperation
Dispute Settlement
Trade Facilitation

Sources: APEC/SOM 2007. *APEC Model Measures for RTAs/FTAs.*

Table 5.2 lists fifteen areas in the APEC model measures for RTAs/FTAs published in 2008 (APEC/SOM 2008). Two to three APEC economies volunteered to work on drafting the model measures for each area and SOM put them together in this form. Its chapeau states that it will be implemented on the APEC principle of voluntariness and no economy will be forced to adopt an FTA because of it. It is produced based on RTAs/FTAs most commonly adopted in the APEC region and drafted in non-legal terms. Individual economies are only expected to refer to it in future FTA negotiations, so that they would converge to as high a level FTA as possible in this region. It was adopted at the APEC conference in Lima in 2008, except for a few areas.

In the process of globalization, many firms — big firms and SMEs (small and medium enterprises) alike — have established their production networks over different economies so that materials, parts, and finished products can move actively across borders. They gain preferential benefits if host economies join the same FTAs, but they have to comply with a set of complicated rules of origin of their products in order to claim the FTA preference. These rules set out the criteria for originating goods: those produced entirely within the economy, provided each non-originating material undergoes an applicable change in tariff classification, or the good satisfies an applicable value content requirement, or undergoes a specified manufacturing or processing operation. Origin procedures either require a certificate by an officially acknowledged third party or only self-certification. They differ in different FTAs so if a firm is engaged in FTAs with different rules of origin, it has to put up with divergent rules of origin and complicated certification procedures. SMEs unaccustomed to this "spaghetti-bowl effect" tend to give up applying for preferential benefits, which results in low utilization ratios by firms in many FTAs. The ABAC proposal insists on similar and simple rules of origin being adopted by RTAs/FTAs in the APEC region.

In 2006, with ABAC's support, the University of California, Marshall School of Business, conducted a detailed check of divergences and convergences of rules of origins in the APEC region, as well as India, and submitted its report to the APEC conference in Sydney in 2007 (USC Marshall School of Business 2007). It produced the Catalogue Rules of Origin regimes of twenty-five FTAs, compared them with APEC's model measures (U.S. version), identified many divergences and some convergences, conducted a detailed interview survey of business executives in the APEC economies, and captured their views on obstacles caused by complicated rules of origin. It took advantage of students in the field study and, in spite of the somewhat mechanical handling, made valid points.

APEC's RTA/FTA model measures mentioned above recommend a set of simplified and harmonized rules of origin. Since these model measures are only a reference and no economy is bound to adopt them, we will just have to observe how they will help RTAs/FTAs converge to a simple and harmonious one in the APEC region. Fortunately we have witnessed a few moves in this direction. In 2008 ASEAN changed its traditional 40 per cent value-added requirement to a new rule in which firms can apply either a 40 per cent value-added requirement or its equivalent tariff-line change. Incidentally the recent revision of ASEAN's CEPT (ASEAN Trade in Goods Agreement, ATIGA 2009) fits well with these APEC model measures. Nine APEC economies reported in their IAPs of 2009 that they have adopted a self-certification practice in applying their rules of origin.

Economic and Technical Cooperation (Ecotech)

APEC has paid due attention to economic cooperation since its inception. At the first APEC Ministerial Meeting in Canberra in 1989, at the ministers' suggestion, senior officials designated seven projects to work on: review of trade and investment data; trade promotion; expansion of investment and technology transfer; Asia-Pacific multilateral human resource development initiatives; regional energy cooperation; marine resource conservation, and telecommunications. At the third APEC Ministerial Meeting in Seoul in November 1991, three more work projects were added in the areas of fisheries, transportation, and tourism, thereby expanding the number of work projects to ten.

Framework of Ecotech

The Osaka Action Agenda (OAA) dealt with economic and technical cooperation (Ecotech) in part two. The Essential Elements of Ecotech stated that as "APEC economies will pursue economic and technical cooperation in order to attain sustainable growth and equitable development in the Asia-Pacific region, while reducing economic disparities among APEC economies and improving the economic and social well-being of all our people" (APEC/MM 1995).

It covered thirteen areas: trade and investment data, trade promotion, industrial science and technology, human resource development, energy, marine resource conservation, fisheries, telecommunications and information, transportation, tourism, SMEs, economic infrastructure, and agricultural technology. Most of them succeeded the earlier projects mentioned above.

The OAA also set a new modality for APEC cooperation. It emphasized the departure from the conventional modality of a distinct donor-recipient relationship. Member governments would contribute on a voluntary basis resources available to them, such as funds, technology, and human skills, and they would all gain from the cooperation programme. Consistency with the market mechanism was emphasized and participation by the private sector was encouraged. However, It has yet to be elaborated how cooperation programmes along these guidelines are to be strengthened.

By 1995 approximately two hundred projects had been proposed as APEC work projects, but they remained as studies and seminars and are yet to be strengthened for visible achievement. At the first SOM in February 1995, the Japanese chair proposed the concept of "Partners for Progress" (PFP), with the intention of making a breakthrough in the hesitation to strengthen the cooperation beyond studies and seminars. It contained an ambitious programme of including a wide range of cooperation activities and establishing a standing agency within APEC to administer them. However, concerns about additional funding and the reluctance to establish a standing agency with personnel cropped up as resistance to the proposal. As it turns out, a cautious start was made with technical cooperation in improving administrative capability and transferring technology in the three TILF areas of standards and conformance, intellectual property rights, and competition policy. These were indispensable for the successful implementation of liberalization and facilitation and were easily agreed upon. Furthermore, Japanese Prime Minister Murayama announced in his speech at the leaders' dinner that Japan would commit to the contribution of 10 billion yen over several years to the promotion of TILF.

The lack of consensus on economic cooperation among APEC economies has impeded the strengthening of cooperation efforts in APEC. This is partly reflected in the frustrations of naming APEC's cooperation programme. President Soeharto refered to "development cooperation" in the Bogor Declaration, but some economies objected to the term. Through the discussion in preparing the OAA in 1995, senior officials finally agreed on the modest term, "economic and technical cooperation".

The Manila Action Plan for APEC (MAPA) Part IV contains the Progress Report on APEC Ecotech Joint Activities. It gives an overview of 320 joint activities and 151 sub-activities under the APEC Ecotech Agenda as of November 1996. While TILF was undertaken by the governments of individual economies (Individual Action Plans, IAPs), and collectively by all economies (Collective Action Plans, CAPs), each activity in Ecotech was coordinated by its lead "shepherd" (mostly from the original proponent of the activity) and participated in by other economies on a voluntary basis. The progress report was constituted from reports on individual activities submitted by individual shepherds.

If compared with conventional, bilateral official development assistance (ODA), these logistical aspects clarify the characteristics of APEC's ecotech (Yamazawa 1998). A typical APEC/ecotech activity is a pet project proposed and coordinated by a member economy, financed mainly by the proponent, and partly supported by APEC's central funds. Out of 104 APEC fund-supported projects, fifty projects received US$20,000–US$50,000, while thirty-six received less than US$20,000, fifteen projects received US$50,000–US$100,000, and only three projects received more than US$100,000. It is basically a technical assistance grant under conventional bilateral ODA, provided by a conventional donor, but of a smaller budget. The average budget size of Japanese technical assistance was 1.4 billion yen (US$11.7

million) for a rice cultivation machine centre in Indonesia, and 2.52 billion yen (US$21 million) for a model pilot plant of cleaner coal burning in China, both in 1996. Although no exact figures are available for the average budget size of an ecotech activity, they may be ten to twenty times as much as the average size of APEC ecotech activities.

Guidance by the Ecotech Subcommittee

The ecotech activities were criticized for their poor visible achievements because they were proposed and implemented on the initiative of individual economies. The MAPA in 1996 set out six priority areas as follows:

- Develop human capital
- Develop stable, safe, and efficient capital markets
- Strengthen economic infrastructure
- Harness technologies for the future
- Safeguard the quality of life through environmentally sound growth
- Develop and strengthen the dynamism of SMEs

In 1997, the Ecotech Subcommittee (ESC) was established to coordinate APEC's expanding ecotech efforts. Guidelines for strengthening ecotech management were established in 1998 and the subcommittee was instructed to submit an annual ECC report to the Ministerial Meeting. The ESC report (APEC/SOM 2000) provides us with a comprehensive review of these ecotech activities in a concise but comparable format. The number of ecotech projects decreased from 200 to 185, while 35 ecotech-related projects under CTI (Committee for Trade and Investment) and other APEC committees have been added. The report confirms recent changes in its focus to concrete cooperation activities, seminars, and training rather than study and research. Human resource development has remained a major focus of ecotech.

The most recent ESC report (2008) indicated the following three directions for its policy guidance:

(A) Top-down framework to guide APEC/ecotech activities
(B) Strategic and long-term approach towards capacity building
(C) Leveraging APEC's partnerships with other multilateral organizations and private sectors

How well have the ecotech forums been reshuffled so far? Tables 5.3–5.5 are based on the 2008 ESC report. The priority areas have increased from six to ten, reflecting new challenges which APEC is facing in the 2000s. The number of ecotech projects funded by APEC was reduced to 77. Some other projects were self-funded by proponent economies. While human resource development was among the prioritized projects as is consistent with the policy guidance (B) above, it is noteworthy that new priority areas such as quality of life and human security are also prioritized in the fund allocation.[6]

Table 5.4 lists all sixteen forums related to the priority areas for which they are pursued. Working groups were reduced to twelve (no. 1–11 and 15), but four task forces (no. 12–14 and 16) were newly established. As is seen in these tables, individual priority areas are pursued across the conventionally classified fora, and they are coordinated with one another

TABLE 5.3
Priority Issues in APEC Ecotech

	Priority Activities	Number of projects funded by APEC
A	Developing human capital	16
B	Developing stable and efficient markets through structural reform	3
C	Strengthening economic infrastructure	2
D	Facilitating technology flows and harnessing technologies for the future	5
E	Safeguarding the quality of life through environmentally sound growth	16
F	Developing and strengthening the dynamism of SMEs	5
G	Integration into the global economy	6
H	Human security and counterterrorism capacity building	17
I	Promoting the development of knowledge-based economies	5
J	Addressing social dimensions of globalization	2
	Total	77

Source: APEC SOM Committee on Ecotech, *2008 Senior Officials' Report on Economic and Technical Cooperation*, November 2008.

TABLE 5.4
Ecotech Activities: Working Groups and Taskforces

	Working Groups and Task Forces	Priority Activities
1	Agricultural and Technical Cooperation Working Group (ATCWG)	B,D,E,G,H
2	Energy Working Group (EWG)	D,E
3	Fisheries Working Group (FWG)	E,F
4	Health Working Group (HWG)	H
5	Human Resources Development Working Group (HRDWG)	A,G,I,J
6	Industrial Science and Technology Working Group (ISTWG)	A,D,E,F,H,J
7	Marine Resource Conservation Working Group (MRCWG)	A,D,E,I
8	Small to Medium Enterprise Working Group (SMEWG)	F,H
9	Telecommunications Working Group (TELWG)	C,G,H,I
10	Transportation Working Group (TPTWG)	A,C,D,E,F,G,H,I
11	Tourism Working Group (TWG)	A,F,G
12	Anti-Corruption and Transparency Task Force (ACT)	B,F
13	Counterterrorism Task Force (CTTF)	A,C,H
14	Gender Focal Point Network (GFPN)	A,F,H,I,J
15	Mining Task Force (MTF)	B,C
16	Task Force for Emergency Preparedness (TFEP)	H

Notes: Refer to Table 5.3 for list of priorities.
Source: APEC SOM Committee on Ecotech, *2008 Senior Officials' Report on Economic and Technical Cooperation*, November 2008.

TABLE 5.5
Ecotech Projects by Type

Types of activity	Number of projects	%
Seminar/Symposium	47	61.03
Training	10	12.98
Survey or analysis and research	16	20.77
Others	4	5.20
Total	77	

Source: APEC SOM Committee on Ecotech, *2008 Senior Officials' Report on Economic and Technical Cooperation*, November 2008.

in pursuance of individual priorities. Individual fora are organized by different ministries responsible for the particular issues in individual economies, so it would be difficult to reshuffle across ministries.

Table 5.5 shows that seminars and symposiums still dominate the type of ecotech activities, which is the result of the strict budgetary constraint mentioned above. However, there is a decrease in surveys and research, but increased training for concrete human resource development. Although the management of the ecotech has remained unchanged, a gradual reshuffling and shift towards new challenges is witnessed.

Need for External Relevance and Support

APEC's ecotech suffers not only from inefficient internal management, but also from a lack of external relevance. The ESC's policy guidance (C) above suggests strengthening links with multilateral organizations such as the World Bank, Asian Development Bank, and the Organization for Economic Cooperation and Development (OECD). This direction should be pursued intently, since they have far greater budgets than APEC. As in TILF, APEC can play the catalyst role best in ecotech activities. Here APEC has to take in the private sector.

Professor Feinberg of the University of California, San Diego, organized a project assessing APEC's activities (APIAN), including ecotech as well as TILF. It includes a sharp review of its human resource development as follows, which is also relevant to other Ecotech areas (Feinberg et al. 2003).

> APEC activities lack relevance or are poorly linked to outside interests. A relatively small group of APEC insiders takes the time to concern themselves with APEC, and when issues do arise, it is not surprising that the ones most energetically pursued reflect the interest of the people in the APEC process. Despite the use of the Ecotech framework, it appears that the goal of increased private sector participation and initiation of activities is not being met. Nor is there much evidence of successful efforts to combine government actions, private sector projects and joint public-private activites with the public sector playing a direct sector initiative. Participation in the APEC process needs to be more attractive to the private sector. The time-consuming nature of APEC procedures, including the onerous guidelines for projects, the impenetrable maze of acronyms, and APEC's organizational structure as well as the high cost of managing APEC projects, all combine to actively discourage private sector participation. (Lu and Taylor 2001)

I share this review based on my own experiences in participating in a few working group meetings and we have not heard that the situation has improved drastically these past years. We have already seen in Chapter 3, that APEC has tried hard to incorporate ABAC into its routine activities. But APEC should also incorporate wider private sector participation, including non-governmental organizations. APEC needs to disseminate its activities and invite wider participation, as well as demonstrate flexible implementation of their intergovernmental consultation framework.

Structural Reform

Liberalization eliminates barriers to trade and investment at national borders, but border barriers are often linked with domestic regulations so that liberalization alone cannot bring free trade and investment. These domestic regulations are called behind-the-border measures and have attracted attention within APEC in the 2000s. It goes without saying that these domestic barriers had been perceived before, as deregulation and competition policies are included in the OAA, but its instruction regarding the two areas is ambiguous and not effectively implemented.

In 2004 in Santiago, APEC leaders highlighted this problem in the Leaders' Agenda to Implement Structural Reform (LAISR), and assigned it to the Economic Committee (see Figure 3.1, chapter 3) (APEC/LM 2004). The Economic Committee had been established in 1994, but conducted academic studies on APEC's priority issues such as TILF. It published such reports as the CGE (computable general equilibrium) Model Analysis of TILF (1999), New Economy and Business Utilizing IT (2000), Promotion of Knowledge-Intensive Economies (2002), and Innovation and Human Resources Availability (2003). In 2006 its chairman from New Zealand made a distinctive move towards structural reform. In the Economic Policy Report (APEC/EC 2006), he identified five priority areas for the structural reform of domestic measures by 2010: competition policy, regulatory reform, public sector governance, corporate governance, and strengthening economic and legal infrastructure. The Economic Committee would pick up these areas one by one and do a stocktaking of their progress by 2010. It also promoted a study of cooperation with OECD, and organized seminars on capacity building of a competition policy.

However, the Economic Committee does not step into the coordination of policy implementation, unlike the CTI. It remains a forum of government officials in charge of economic policy, promotes exchange of information regarding structural reforms in individual economies, and provides opportunities for discussion. It also takes charge of the overview of the current state of the APEC economies.

Notes

1. Incidentally, the ASEAN Economic Community Blueprint (ASEAN 2008), published by the ASEAN Secretariat in 2008, also detailed an annual schedule for implementing its policy measures for achieving its economic community, which I found to be similar to the Hanoi Action Plan. The latter came out two years later and I regard it as evidence of ASEAN learning from APEC practices.
2. Because of the difference of this new type of agreement from ordinary FTAs, APEC refers to RTAs/FTAs in its official statement. However, my reference to FTAs includes both types.
3. Please refer to Chapter 7 for a detailed argument for the Japanese FTA strategy.
4. I served as president of the Institute of Developing Economies/JETRO from 1998–2003 and conducted a joint preparatory study on the Japan-Korea FTA with the Korea Institute for International Economic Policy (KIEP) in 1999–2000, and a joint study of the ASEAN-Japan CEP (comprehensive economic partnership) with ten ASEAN research institutes in 2003. Although working outside the ambit of the Japanese Government, I felt obliged to defend the government's policy (IDE/JETRO 2000, Yamazawa 2000, IDE/JETRO 2003).
5. Incidentally, the EPG Report III (APEC/EPG 1995) had made the same recommendation under the title of "Toward Open Sub-Regionalism" (pp. 29–37 and 58). It had preceded the following argument among PECC, ABAC, and APEC by almost ten years, but was never taken up, partly because of its suggestion of negotiating for liberalization.
6. These new priority areas are detailed in Chapter 6.

6

Towards the Free Trade Area of the Asia-Pacific (FTAAP)

We have seen APEC's progress in its main activity, trade investment liberalization and facilitation in Chapters 2, 4, and 5. APEC met its mid-term Bogor Goals in 2010 and has started to tackle the post-Bogor agenda, that is, to pursue deeper liberalization and facilitation in the form of FTAAP and the Trans-Pacific Strategic Partnership (TPP), as well as broader cooperation in pursuit of greater economic growth.

In 2006 the APEC Business Advisory Council (ABAC) proposed a greater free trade area (FTA) covering all of the APEC economies (ABAC 2006). It aimed to promote the integration of all the FTAs that had mushroomed in the region over the past decade, thus creating a greater single market to achieve the maximum scale economy. The joint ABAC/Pacific Economic Cooperation Council (PECC) report of the same year (ABAC/PECC 2006) included both pros and cons of the FTAAP. Fred Bergsten, Director of the Peterson Institute of International Economics, Washington D.C., expressed his concern about the hobbled negotiations of the World Trade Organization (WTO)/Doha Development Agenda (DDA), and recommended FTAAP as a "Plan B" in preparation for the failure of the DDA and resulting vacuum of liberalization momentum in the region (Bergsten 2006). On the other hand, Charles Morrison, the

American Chair of PECC, represented a majority view of PECC academics, indicating practical difficulty in conducting liberalization negotiations within APEC and insisting on the pragmatic strategy of the Busan Roadmap (Morrison 2006).

Bergsten served as the chair of APEC/EPG (Eminent Persons Group) from 1993 to 1995 and actively led the liberalization momentum within APEC then. The momentum heightened to the Bogor Declaration in 1994 and he planned to achieve it by negotiating an FTA (see Chapter 2 for details). However, in the following year the Japanese host invented the concept of "concerted unilateral liberalization" (CUL) within the Osaka Action Agenda, which disappointed many Americans, including Bergsten. I conjecture that after ten years he has resumed his original proposal together with American ABAC members. Of course FTAAP implies that APEC should quit its CUL modality and convert it to a legally binding FTA.

FTAAP continued to be discussed in the APEC Study Center conference in Melbourne in May 2007. I was invited to discuss its possibility together with Bergsten in the same session. I supported his suggestion of promoting FTAAP as a Plan B in case of the failure of DDA. I also attracted the participants' attention to the increased momentum for the East Asian Community and suggested that both the East Asia Free Trade Area (EAFTA) and FTAAP could be promoted in parallel (Yamazawa 2008). After all, APEC Leaders agreed to continue to study "a possible Free Trade Area of the Asia-Pacific in the long term", as stated in the subtitle of its report *The APEC Initiative for Strengthening Regional Integration* (APEC 2007).

Nevertheless, the current studies of FTAAP have not developed concrete procedures for achieving it. Academic studies focused on the computable general equilibrium (CGE) model calculations under specific assumptions, which result in greater welfare gains of FTA of a greater geographical coverage. Sangkyom Kim (2009) reported that under the assumption of all tariffs abolished, a 10 per cent reduction of services barriers, a 5 per cent reduction of transaction cost through trade facilitation, and simplified rules of origin, all APEC economies would gain and APEC's real GDP would increase by 1.13 per cent, while the real GDP of the European Union would decrease by 0.08 per cent and that of the rest of the world decrease by 0.06 per cent. Since welfare gains are in the order of 0.1 per cent or less for smaller FTAs, FTAAP would lead to greater trade creation but less trade diversion effects.

For the past few years FTAAP has been "translated from an aspiration to a more concrete vision". The DDA negotiations have been halted for the past five years, so the Plan B is still relevant. The 2010 APEC Leaders' Declaration included an appendix entitled "Pathway to FTAAP" (APEC/LM 2010*c*) clarifying its vision:

> FTAAP should do more than achieve liberalization in its narrow sense; it should be comprehensive, high quality and incorporate and address next generation trade and investment issues.
>
> It should be pursued as a comprehensive FTA by developing and building on ongoing regional undertakings such as ASEAN+3, ASEAN+6, and TPP. To this end APEC will make an important meaningful contribution as an incubator of a FTAAP by providing leadership and intellectual input into the process.

APEC should keep the modality of its non-binding nature and voluntarism, continue progress towards achieving the Bogor Goals within APEC economies by 2020, and at the same time work more actively towards addressing non-tariff or behind-the-border barriers and other next-generation trade and investment issues to further deepen economic integration in the region. Effective eco-technology should be provided so as to help APEC developing economies to improve their capacity for further trade and investment liberalization and facilitation (TILF) and meet new challenges (APEC LM 2010*c*). Although the leaders did not specify a deadline for accomplishing a FTAAP, we should not halt the TILF process but convert it to a binding FTAAP at the time of the Bogor Goals in 2020.

Trans-Pacific Partnership

On the other hand, the TPP has emerged as a binding FTA among a select group of APEC economies, eventually leading to the FTAAP, as suggested above. TPP was originally formed by the four APEC economies of Brunei, Chile, New Zealand, and Singapore in 2006. Its objective in Article 1 states that it aims to "establish a Trans-Pacific Strategic Economic Partnership among the parties, based on common interest and deepening of the relationship in all areas of application". It has taken a "WTO plus" approach, covering not only commodity and services trade but also such facilitation areas as rules of origin, customs procedures, trade remedies, technical barriers to trade, competition policy, intellectual property, government procurement, and dispute settlement (TPP 2006).

The evolution of TTP originated in the late 1990s when some APEC economies were disappointed by the stalled move for liberalization within APEC (see Chapter 2). The like-minded economies of Australia, New Zealand, the United States, Singapore, and Chile started the P5 talks on the occasion of APEC meetings in order to find a path towards further liberalization. While the United States and Australia dropped out, the remaining P3 conducted four rounds of negotiations in 2002–05 and announced their TPSEP (Trans-Pacific Strategic Economic Partnership) Agreement at the APEC/Ministers Responsible for Trade (MRT) meeting in 2005. Brunei joined at the last minute to form the P4 (Elms 2010). In late 2008 the United States expressed interest in participating in TPP and started negotiation for the expansion together with Australia, Peru, and Vietnam in March 2010.

The number of current participants in the TPP negotiations does not promise a sufficient merit of scale. Table 6.1 presents the trade intensity indices for the eight economies negotiating the expansion of TPP. Of the four original member economies, Brunei and Singapore have had a high intensity and New Zealand and Singapore have doubled the intensity between the two, while so far Chile has had little trade with the other three. Even after the United States and the other three economies join, traditional close trade between Australia and New Zealand, Singapore and Vietnam, and Chile and Peru will be distinguished, but rather remoter trans-pacific trade would result between Asia-Oceania and America. P4 accounts for only 1.63 per cent of APEC in the total gross domestic product, seven economies other than the United States account for 5.5 per cent. These figures do not support a strong case for the eight-economy TPP. Besides, the United States has already concluded FTAs with Australia, Chile, Peru, and Singapore, so that further expansion to the eight-economy TPP will not provide much additional room for expansion of trade and investment.

The current TPP negotiations are being conducted by nine APEC economies, adding Malaysia as a new participant. They have been held every three months in one of the participating economies in turn. What the new TTP will be like has not been publicized yet, but it is understood that the high-level FTA of the original P4 will be extended to its final form, that is, to abolish tariffs and non-tariff measures in almost all

TABLE 6.1
Trade Intensity Indices of the TPP Economies, 1995 and 2007

	Brunei	Singapore	New Zealand	Chile	USA	Peru	Australia	Vietnam
Brunei		3.93	—	0	0.11	0.94	0.67	—
		1.06	9.32	0	0.42	0	12.21	—
Singapore	17.9		1.18	0.23	1.20	0.12	1.94	6.51
	8.9		2.57	0.10	0.64	0.06	3.39	4.47
New Zealand	1.16	0.57		1.37	0.65	2.83	17.93	1.22
	0.31	1.12		0.49	0.84	0.69	19.92	2.05
Chile	—	0.20	0.34		0.99	18.06	0.33	—
	—	0.10	0.19		0.94	11.67	0.38	0.34
USA	0.47	1.07	1.05	1.97		2.01	1.63	0.19
	0.46	1.34	1.20	2.36		2.63	1.50	0.34
Peru	—	0.01	0.07	8.76	1.13		0.17	0.15
	—	0.01	0.20	20.28	1.39		0.32	0.36
Australia	1.29	2.19	26.47	0.64	0.42	0.18		1.24
	0.70	1.43	27.82	0.39	0.44	0.37		1.74
Vietnam	—	2.91	0.51	—	0.22	1.27	3.29	
	—	2.72	0.68	0.32	1.52	0.25	7.09	

Note: The first four economies formed the TPP in 2006, while the last four economies are currently applying for membership.

sectors in ten years. The addition of further participants, such as Japan, Canada, and South Korea, is often mentioned. Prime Minister Kan planned to announce Japan's accession officially at the Leaders' Meeting so as to make it a highlight of APEC 2010 in Yokohama, but he had to postpone it due to strong resistance by agricultural cooperatives and the lack of nationwide consensus on it. Neither Canada nor South Korea have applied for TPP yet, partly because they are already engaged in a FTA with the United States. Canada has been an FTA partner with the United States (North American Free Trade Agreement [NAFTA] since 1994) and South Korea signed an FTA in 2008 which is waiting ratification by the U.S. Congress.

Nevertheless, the TPP negotiations require difficult adjustments at home for individual participating economies. The United States stressed its intention of formulating broader high-level regional integration through TPP (USTR Report 2010) and has taken a strong initiative in promoting the negotiations, sticking to its NAFTA modality. However, the Obama administration is severely constrained by minority power in Congress. Original P4 members, Australia and Peru, have experienced difficult adjustments to strong demands by the United States in their past FTA negotiations and wish to avoid similar experiences (Scollay 2010). Vietnam and Malaysia anticipate difficult adjustment at home through joining the TPP.

What difficulty in adjusting does Japan face at home? Prime Minister Kan proposed the TPP as a symbol of the "third country opening"; as Japan's economy and society have matured it has become inward looking. Japan should join the TPP in order to arrest this process and promote active advancement overseas. Japanese firms cannot survive global competition only at the domestic market with an aged population and fewer children, resulting in weakened dynamism. They have to move out to growing neighbouring markets in Asia. It is imperative to produce a seamless business environment in which both Japanese and other Asian firms can conduct free and stable business. This will lead to an East Asian Community. The Ministry of Economy, Trade, and Industry (METI) has been addressing neighbouring Asian economies in its series of white papers on international trade over the last few years. Joining TPP should lead eventually to this Asia Pacific–wide market.

The Japanese Federation of Economic Organizations (Keidanren) and other business leaders readily supported this initiative, followed by representative labour unions. Keidanren has been contending that "Japan will be discriminated and left behind the globalization trend if she does not join TPP". METI supported their contention with a calculation emphasizing "the cost of not joining TPP". This is the domino theory of FTAs or competitive liberalization which urges you to "join as your neighbours do". Once a member one can "gain from trade diversion by discriminating non-members".

On the other hand, agricultural cooperatives and parliamentary members elected from agricultural constituencies — groups with vested interests in maintaining the long-established protective subsidies — organized a nationwide protest against the TPP move, saying that it would ruin Japanese agriculture and rural life and insisting that Japan should maintain its economic partnership agreement strategy, under which rice and major crops are exempted from liberalization. However, the fact is that the number of Japanese farmers has decreased by 25 per cent over the past decade due to ageing and the difficulty of finding successors under the current protective policy. Reform for competitive agriculture is imperative, regardless of whether Japan joins TPP or not. As a matter of fact, vegetable and fruit growers operating outside the protection have already achieved competitive production and have not joined this protest movement. Our opinion group proposed to Prime Minister Aso a programme of nurturing competitive farmers without protection two years ago, but received no response (Japan Forum for International Relations, *The 31st Policy Recommendations: Japan's Strategy for Its Agriculture in the Globalized World*, January 2009). We witness the need to reform Japanese institutions and practices in a number of areas in addition to agriculture, but strong political leadership is blocked by huge vested-interest groups.

Nevertheless, cautious attitudes towards FTAAP are still held in Asia. Other ASEAN (Association of Southeast Asian Nations) members — Indonesia, the Philippines, and Thailand — are not interested in the TPP negotiations. They did not volunteer to be assessed at the mid-term Bogor Goals and remain to be assessed in 2020. But they have made fair progress in the TILF process (Chapter 4), achieved ASEAN Free Trade Area (AFTA) liberalization, and are working towards the 2015 target for the ASEAN Economic Community. On the other hand, China has fulfilled the liberalization required of its accession to the WTO in 2001, which has paved the way to the globalization of the Chinese economy and firms.

Nevertheless, as we saw in Chapter 4, the country's economic regime still retains various forms of governmental regulations and the Chinese Government is cautious about the process of deregulation. China is afraid of conceding to aspects of the NAFTA modality, such as labour standards and human rights in the TPP negotiations. Furthermore, the security stances of China and the United States stand opposed to each other. China feels excluded from the TPP and prefers liberalization in East Asia under ASEAN+3.[1]

APEC member economies insist that the grouping should maintain its conventional modality of voluntarism, consensus building, and non-binding approach, but not admit any negotiations for liberalization. I believe it is necessary for APEC to gradually introduce a binding element, as I referred to the late Hadi Soesastro's remark of "from v-APEC to b-APEC" in Chapter 2 (p. 14). Major ASEAN members have developed the market economy for the past two decades and China acceded to the WTO regime a decade ago. The recent Greek crisis and the resulting disturbance in Europe tells us that if we wish to build an East Asian Economic Community, its member economies need to be disciplined so as to implement proper economic policies, and we need to start moving in that direction now. TPP is expected to provide us with a role model for disciplined economic management. FTAAP will come along as an extension.

It is difficult for APEC to work on the FTAAP now since it is not set to negotiate liberalization among members. However, thanks to the pathfinder approach adopted in 2003, some prepared members can go ahead to implement a project in advance and other members can join later. APEC can pursue FTAAP along this pathfinder approach. The United States and other TPP participants prefer a strategy of strengthening APEC liberalization while working on TPP outside of APEC. First TPP will establish a model for deeper liberalization among prepared economies and invite the rest of the APEC economies to join in changing TPP to FTAAP later (USTR 2011, pp. 140–41).

To conclude, the trade-offs of the TPP negotiations have been the high-level FTA and the economy of scale of including China and other ASEAN countries. If it continues with the NAFTA modality under the U.S. initiative, the result will be trans-Pacific but will divide Asia. Of course, the United States contends that she will never exclude China, but expects that China will achieve further liberalization in the future and join the TPP (Petri 2010; USTR 2011). However, we cannot delay the conclusion of

FTAAP for long after 2020. We hope that the current promoters of TPP will be clever enough to balance the trade-off. In this regard, Japan should join the TPP negotiations at an early stage and guide it in that direction. Besides, it will help the nation if she works to strengthen the continued TILF process within APEC.

APEC's Growth Strategy

While APEC economies, especially emerging economy members, have achieved high growth for the past two decades, they also face various challenges affecting their future growth paths: macroeconomic imbalances with the outside world, increasing income disparity, weak governance of public and private institutions, environmental degradation, natural disasters and epidemics, etc. APEC has responded to meet them with new eco-technology forums and task forces and the leaders' initiative for structural reform (see Chapter 5). These have become a major workload for APEC in addition to its main agenda of TILF, which has necessitated senior officials to reprioritize them as a major post-Bogor agenda. In APEC 2009 in Singapore, the Leaders' Joint Declaration called for joint efforts by member economies to pursue a new growth paradigm in Asia Pacific cooperation for the twenty-first century, promoting "strong, continuous and balanced growth", "inclusive growth", and "sustainable growth". In APEC 2010 in Yokohama, the leaders formulated the "APEC Leaders' Growth Strategy" (APEC/LM 2010*c*), which consists of the following five attributes:

- Balanced Growth: We seek growth across and within our economies through macroeconomic policies and structural reforms that will gradually unwind imbalances and raise potential output.
- Inclusive Growth: We seek to ensure that all our citizens have the opportunity to participate in, contribute to, and benefit from global economic growth.
- Sustainable Growth: We seek growth compatible with global efforts for protection of the environment and transition to green economies.
- Innovative Growth: We seek to create an economic environment and promote innovation and emerging economic sectors.
- Secure Growth: We seek to protect the region's citizens' economic and physical well-being and to provide the secure environment necessary for economic activity.

In regard to its action plan, the leaders identified five critical integrated work elements: structural reform, human resources and entrepreneurship development, green growth, knowledge-based economy, and human security. They instructed APEC senior officials to "play a central, coordinating, and guiding role in this process". Senior officials "should implement this Action Plan, conducting annual progress reviews on APEC's relevant work programs", and "report to Leaders in 2015 for their review".

These are further Bogor Goals for APEC's growth strategy, with a mid-term deadline of 2015. They are a comprehensive list of growth attributes that will make high economic growth for the Asia-Pacific worthy and credible. No one will deny the importance of the five attributes, and it is quite timely that APEC seeks to tackle them in the year when APEC leaders reviewed their mid-term progress towards achievement of the Bogor Goals. However, it is not clear from the Leaders' Declaration (APEC/LM 2010*c*) how, beyond mere lip service, they will be effectively implemented as the post-Bogor agenda. The task devolves to APEC 2011 and the U.S. host. We may need a Honolulu Action Agenda to effectively implement the APEC Growth Strategy, just as the Osaka Action Agenda was adopted to achieve the Bogor Goals fifteen years ago. The sections that follow suggest possible directions.

Macro-Economic and Financial Cooperation

In order to address balanced growth we need closer cooperation among APEC economies in macroeconomic policies and financial areas. This is not a new agenda but APEC has not so far made any visible achievement in these areas. However, we expect APEC to play a greater role in it hereafter.

The Ministerial Meeting responsible for macroeconomic policy and finance (APEC/FM), delayed by the meeting for trade and investment, started in 1996, and encountered the Asian currency crisis in 1997–98. However, the Finance Ministers' Meeting for ASEAN+3 has played a distinct role and preceded APEC/FM in implementing such concrete measures as the Chiang Mai Initiative (CMI) for bilateral currency swap, and subsequently its multilateralization, nurturing an Asian bond market, and preparing early warning measures for macroeconomic policy. While the same ministry people are participating in both APEC and ASEAN+3, ASEAN+3 seems to have been utilized more readily than APEC for the following reasons. First, ASEAN+3 moved quicker to respond to the currency crisis among Asian members directly affected by it. Second, the United States had a bigger voice in APEC and tended to invite stronger guidance from the International Monetary Fund (IMF). Thailand, Indonesia, South Korea, and other Asian economies that resorted to strict contraction policies under the IMF's directive and experienced aggravated depression, tended to avoid further engagement with the IMF within APEC's financial cooperation. The ASEAN Secretariat serving ASEAN+3, though, does not have financial experts, so the Asian Development Bank (ADB) helps ASEAN+3 in this area.[2]

On the other hand, APEC/FM has been held every year since 1996 but could not provide any effective rescue to ASEAN members and South Korea hit by the currency crisis, which tended to reduce their expectation for APEC. Although with duplicated members, APEC/FM has merely followed ASEAN+3 in CMI and the Asian bond market, and endorsed the latter's implementation in the 2000s.

However, in November 2008, APEC responded in a timely manner to the expanding global economic crisis. In the G-20 Leaders' Summit held on 15 November in Washington DC, leaders decided to take urgent measures to stabilize financial markets and to carry out coordinated macroeconomic policies to restore growth and stability. In the following week, at the APEC Leaders' Meeting in Lima, Peru, the "Lima APEC Leaders' Statement on the Global Economy" (APEC 2008*a*; 2008*b*) was issued. In the statement, APEC leaders strongly supported the Washington Declaration of the G-20 leaders and their action plan. APEC leaders were committed to take broad policy responses needed to overcome the current crisis within eighteen months and reiterated their firm belief that free market principles and open trade and investment regimes should be the measures to continue to drive growth, employment, and poverty reduction. Although APEC/FM used to be held either in February or March at a separate timing from APEC/LM, it was organized conveniently just before APEC/LM.

In 2009 as well, APEC/FM was organized in Singapore just before the APEC/LM, and the heads of the World Bank, IMF, Asian Development Bank (ADB), and ABAC participated in it. Facing the worst financial crisis and global depression, APEC Finance Ministers, with the size and dynamism of the APEC economies, agreed to support the G-20 in active fiscal policies, strengthening the financial system, and securing finance for sustaining growth (APEC/FM 2009).

Globalization proceeds quickly in fiscal and financial areas, and the Lehman shock of 2008 and the Greek crisis and disturbance in Europe in 2010 quickly spread to East Asia. East Asia must join other regions in tackling the global crisis. It also has its own problems with the macroeconomy and finance.

First, it has to avoid a recurrence of the 1997–98 Asian currency crisis. East Asian economies organized a bilateral currency swap network to meet the emergency. This developed into a multilateral network in 2009.

Second, the Chinese renminbi needs to appreciate against the U.S. dollar from its current rate, which has been pegged almost since the Asian currency crisis in response to the rapid growth of the Chinese economy and huge accumulation of her exchange reserve. It would not only solve the China-U.S. conflict but would also serve to stabilize the currency system, including the Japanese yen and other Asian currencies. An Asian common currency is a long-term goal, but we need to build currency cooperation in this direction.

Third, we still face a huge imbalance of the global macroeconomy, which should be addressed. We have long been warned against a possible break resulting from persistent deficit of the U.S. current account and accumulated surplus on the side of China, Japan, and other Asian economies. Asian economies need to reform their economic structure of continuing growth based on exports to the U.S. market and change to growth based on domestic demand, enabling their consumers to enjoy the benefits of high growth. It requires not only domestic policy efforts by individual economies but also coordinated policy by all economies in our world of a production network covering the whole of East Asia.

We expect that these problems for East Asia can be handled swiftly and effectively, not by the IMF and the Europe-based Financial Stability Board, but through initiatives from East Asia. The first problem mentioned above was solved by ASEAN+3, not under the ASEAN initiative but by that of the Plus Three. The second and third problems cannot be tackled by ASEAN+3 alone, but require coordinated efforts from several parties, including the United States. APEC can play an important role in areas of the macroeconomy and finance, taking advantage of financial experts of the ADB. The United States participates in both APEC and the ADB.

In October 2010 the G-20 Summit was held in Seoul in the week preceding APEC Yokohama. The leaders discussed the "beggar thy neighbour" effect of popular monetary easing by developed economies after the Lehman shock and the European crisis, causing excessive inflows of hot money to emerging economies and appreciating their currencies. In February 2011, the G-20 Finance Ministers discussed in Paris whether to set numerical targets for their fiscal policies and exchange rate adjustment so as to ensure their effective coordination. They agreed on the desirable direction, but only as a non-binding commitment without numerical targets because of the reluctance of China and other emerging members. We hope that APEC/FM will play a catalyst role in this direction.[3]

Inclusive Growth and Social Resilience

Inclusive growth is the newest agenda of APEC, which refers to enabling many people to enjoy the benefit of economic growth. It has been pointed out that in the midst of accelerated globalization in the Asia Pacific, an increasing number of people are left behind.

This concept has recently been taken up outside APEC as well. A World Bank report (2009) published a new strategic vision combining "growth and productive employment" with its conventional strategy for poverty reduction. While large developing economies like China, India, and Brazil are developing rapidly, the aim of the report is to modify the conventional focus on income redistribution. An approach has emerged among academic circles that seeks to incorporate welfare state practices into the development of the East Asian Community, instead of hastening economic community building focused on liberalization.

PECC Japan National Committee started a new group study of "inclusive growth and social resilience" in support of the 2010 Japan APEC focus on the APEC Growth Strategy. They conducted a comprehensive survey of East Asian readiness for tackling social resilience (pension scheme, health insurance, and unemployment), human security, and climate change (PECC 2010). As an example, Yasuhiro Kamimura reported on a comparative review of social welfare regimes in East Asian economies. Japan, South Korea, Chinese Taipei, Thailand, China, and Vietnam are equipped with both pensions and insurance, while Singapore, Hong Kong, and other ASEAN members have not implemented unemployment insurance yet. The provision of a social welfare regime does not necessarily reflect the economic conditions, but is also affected by the political acceptance of labour unions, resulting in a wide variety within East Asia.

Nobody denies the importance of inclusive growth. APEC's approach in disseminating best practices and providing assistance in capacity building will help to spread it over the region. We hope that these studies will be upgraded to the implementation of necessary measures over the APEC region.

Broader Regional Cooperation

The APEC Growth Strategy not only deals with all of the issues mentioned above, but also covers a broader geographical area beyond APEC member nations. There exist quite a few emerging economies in the neighbourhood of APEC, in South Asia and the Pacific Islands, that suffer from poverty, environmental degradation, infectious diseases, and natural disasters common to APEC economies. Some of them have formulated their own regional cooperation groups, but suffer from a lack of the necessary capability and administrative governance. APEC, with its major developed and emerging economy members, is expected to cover them.

The G-20 Summit has emerged as the new framework underlying management of the global economy, but it needs to be supported by APEC and other major regional groups in order to ensure that the goals of the G-20 are achieved. Nine APEC economies participate in the G-20, thus providing a driving force for the framework. Mid-sized APEC economies — such as Australia, Indonesia, and South Korea — have participated in the global governance of the G-20 for the first time and are willing to continue to contribute. How can APEC provide a useful framework for their contribution?

APEC has not only been a framework for consensus building over policy coordination among members, but also in providing assistance to developing economy members by way of technology transfers and capacity building. In addition, advantages accrue from overlapping. The G-20 will be tasked in future with such global issues as environmental protection, disaster management, infectious disease prevention, antiterrorism, poverty eradication, and so on. These issues have already been addressed in the APEC framework. Nevertheless, APEC is expected to contribute by cooperating closely with the G-20 to meet these challenges.

The United Nations and its affiliated international organizations have already tackled some of these issues requiring broader cooperation: the World Bank and the United Nations Conference on Trade and Development on poverty reduction, the World Health Organization on epidemics, International Atomic Energy Commission (IAEG) on energy and nuclear, and Conference of the Parties (COP) on climate change. APEC's major members have participated individually in these multilateral forums and acquired experience and capacity. We expect that APEC through its eco-technology forums and taskforces will serve as a catalyst for multilateral cooperation in the Asia Pacific.

Let us review how APEC has taken up a new issue of "emergency preparedness" in recent years. With globalized information and telecommunications, we hear almost every month of occurrences of large natural disasters in various parts of the world. We still remember the 1995 Great Hanshin-Awaji Earthquake, the 2004 Indian Ocean tsunami, the 2008 Sichuan earthquake in China, typhoons and floods in the Philippines, volcanic eruptions, devastating wildfires, and so on. Sometimes central or local governments directly hit by these disasters cannot manage rescue and recovery operations on their own, and may request help from their neighbours or broader international cooperation.

The APEC Leaders' Statement took up the issue of preparing for the emergent needs of rescue and recovery in the wake of large natural disasters. Busan APEC/LM (2005) declared the need for "protecting our economies by taking action to lessen the impact from future disasters and improve our collective response capability". The Hanoi Declaration had this to say: "Recognizing that large-scale natural disasters that affect one economy can affect all of us, we urged member economies to further intensify cooperation, including with the private sector, to maximize regional available resources in order to better prepare the region for disasters and post-disaster rehabilitation and reconstruction" (APEC/LM 2006). In June 2005, the APEC Task Force on Emergency Preparedness (TFEP) was established under joint Australian-Indonesian chairmanship.[4]

The Task Force focused on taking stock of best practices of preparedness for natural disasters and capacity building for rescue and reconstruction, including the mobilization of personnel and resources available from the public and private sectors. It then embarked on Disaster Risk Reduction (DRR), aiming to mitigate the impact of the increasingly frequent, intense, and large-scale disasters as well as disaster management training. Chinese Taipei has been eager in these activities and has organized workshops in 2008 and 2009 which saw participation by fifteen to sixteen economies. The third CEO Forum on disaster management was organized in Hanoi in

September 2009 and the fourth was hosted by Kobe in January 2010. Thailand, Russia, China, and Singapore had also planned to organize workshops and seminars on different issues in 2010.

Notes

1. Hong Kong and Chinese Taipei are well prepared for the TPP negotiations. Both have made far better progress in the TILF process (Chapter 4) and volunteered for the 2010 mid-term Bogor assessment. They are however reserved in expressing their intentions towards China clearly.
2. The author is grateful to Masahiro Kawai, Director, ADB Institute Tokyo, for this information.
3. G-7 FM still maintains its function in coordinating necessary financial cooperation. On 18 March 2011, against the speculative move to the appreciation of the Japanese yen at the time of the Great East Japan Earthquake and nuclear power plant accident, G-7 Finance Ministers cooperated with their Japanese counterparts in coordinated intervention in their own exchange markets, selling yen and buying dollars, and succeeded in reversing the move.
4. The author owes this part of the chapter to the report by Sophia Y.L. Lee, "APEC The Next Decade: Current Status and Future Development of Task Force for Emergency preparedness", delivered at the APEC Study Center Conference in Taipei, December 2009.

7

Paradigm Shift in Asia Pacific Cooperation

The East Asian Community (EAC) has now become popular in the Asia Pacific region, but in the 1990s APEC was the core of regional cooperation. The paradigm of regional cooperation has shifted from APEC to the East Asian Community over the past ten years. The Japanese Government now gives the East Asian Community the highest priority in its regional strategy. In 2002 Prime Minister Koizumi concluded the Japan-Singapore EPA (Economic Partnership Agreement, a free trade agreement [FTA] with a greater coverage than commodity trade) and started the prevalence of FTA/EPA in East Asia. In 2009 Prime Minister Hatoyama sets his core diplomatic strategy on building the East Asian Community.

Nevertheless, the East Asian Community cannot be achieved easily. It certainly has its economic basis, but not its political and security basis yet, and its relationship with the United States and other extra-regional partners cannot be easily seen. On the contrary, APEC provides some elements missing in the building of the East Asian Community. APEC should be utilized for this rather than abandoned. This chapter discusses how to utilize APEC for the sake of East Asian Community building.

Figure 7.1 compares progress over time of regional integration in Europe, the Americas, and East Asia. In Europe, the European Economic Community began in the late 1950s and expanded to become the European

FIGURE 7.1
Paradigm Shift from APEC to EAC

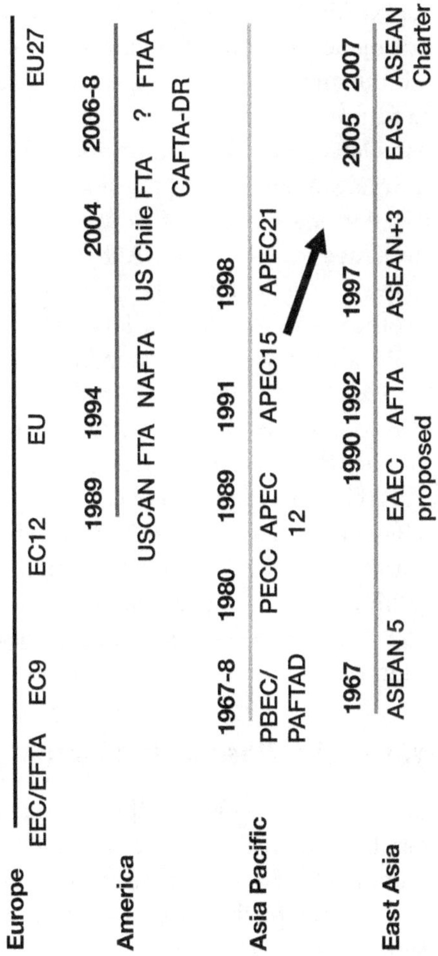

Europe
1958 EEC/EFTA — **1972** EC9 — **1986** EC12 — **1993** EU — **2007** EU27

America
1989 USCAN FTA — **1994** NAFTA — **2004** US Chile FTA — **2006-8** ? FTAA, CAFTA-DR

Asia Pacific
1967-8 PBEC/ PAFTAD — **1980** PECC — **1989** APEC 12 — **1991** APEC15 — **1998** APEC21

East Asia
1967 ASEAN 5 — **1990** EAEC proposed — **1992** AFTA — **1997** ASEAN+3 — **2005** EAS — **2007** ASEAN Charter

Union, with a common trade policy, a single central bank, and a common currency, in 1993. In 2007 it included East European countries to become a twenty-seven-country group. In North America, the United States and Canada — with a common language and intensive trade and investments across a long border — formed an FTA in 1989, and in 1994 added Mexico to become the North American Free Trade Area (NAFTA). The United States has made bilateral FTAs with Chile, Peru, and five Central American countries, with the aim of developing a Free Trade Area of the Americas (FTAA) in the future.[1]

East Asia is a latecomer to this move for regional integration. It started with APEC, a weak institution for regional cooperation. After the Asian currency crisis the Association of Southeast Asian Nations (ASEAN) initiated a Plus Three initiative (ASEAN+3), including China, Japan, and South Korea. It will move towards an East Asian Community in the future. On the other hand, Australia, New Zealand, the United States, and Canada, despite all being APEC members from the start, have not participated in ASEAN+3. They are critical of ASEAN+3 and suggest it should be open to external partners. Australian Prime Minister Rudd's 2008 proposal for an Asia-Pacific Community is consistent with this direction (Rudd 2008). President Obama delivered his Asian policy address in Tokyo in 2009 in which he expressed the U.S. interest in joining the East Asian Summit (Obama 2009). In East Asia, cross-border trade and investment will proceed before the institutionalization of regional integration via FTAs, but we have to see how these external countries will react to the regional economic integration in East Asia.

Moves towards the East Asian Community

While APEC suffered a setback with the Asian currency crisis, East Asian regional cooperation has been enhanced since 1997–98. Most evident is the Chiang Mai Initiative (CMI), a package of currency and financial measures to prevent a recurrence of the currency crisis, which includes currency swap agreements in an emergency, an Asian Bond market, and an early warning system. During the rapid growth period of the East Asian miracle before the crisis, East Asian governments pegged their currencies with the U.S. dollar individually and promoted capital liberalization thanks to the stable currency value. They simply did not need such cooperation before the crisis. The CMI was agreed upon by ten ASEAN members and China, Japan, and South Korea, the so-called ASEAN+3 group.

On the other hand, institutional integration has proceeded in the region. Bilateral FTAs have been concluded both within the region and with outside partners: Japan-Singapore, Singapore-Australia, Thailand-India, Thailand-Australia, Singapore–South Korea, Japan-Malaysia, Japan-Thailand, Japan-Philippines, and Japan-Indonesia. Furthermore, China, Japan, and South Korea have concluded FTAs/EPAs with ASEAN as a whole, the so-called ASEAN+1 type. However, ASEAN+3 has attracted attention as a core institution in the region. Its joint statement was announced at the ASEAN+3 Summit meeting in 2001 and the East Asian Community idea was proposed by the East Asian Vision Group (EAVG) at the ASEAN+3 Summit (EAVG 2001).

ASEAN has taken an initiative in East Asian cooperation. Begun in 1967 with five countries (Indonesia, Malaysia, the Philippines, Thailand, and Singapore), it had made a few achievements in political and diplomatic negotiation with outside partners, but not much in economic areas such as preferential trade agreements or common industrial projects. In 1992 ASEAN started to implement a large scale tariff reduction, AFTA, towards effective regional integration. The association has created concentric circles of cooperation such as ASEAN+1 and ASEAN +3, with ASEAN as the core and in the driver's seat. ASEAN+3 saw the implementation of the Chiang Mai Initiative.

Here ASEAN has taken advantage of its unique formula of the ASEAN Post Ministerial Conference (ASEAN PMC). While ASEAN organized its Economic and Trade Ministers meeting every year, it has started since the late 1980s to invite counterpart ministers of such partner countries as Japan, China, South Korea, and Australia, to negotiate as a group with individual partners, along the ASEAN+1 formula. ASEAN extended this formula to summit meetings so that it could easily organize ASEAN+3 and ASEAN+1 summits taking advantage of the presence of leaders of partner countries. This was a big success for ASEAN diplomacy. China, Japan, and South Korea have all accepted this ASEAN initiative.

While hosting the ASEAN Summit in 2005, Malaysia organized the first East Asia Summit (EAS) by inviting an additional three countries — Australia, New Zealand, and India — and discussed broader regional cooperation on such issues as antiterrorism, recovery from natural disasters,

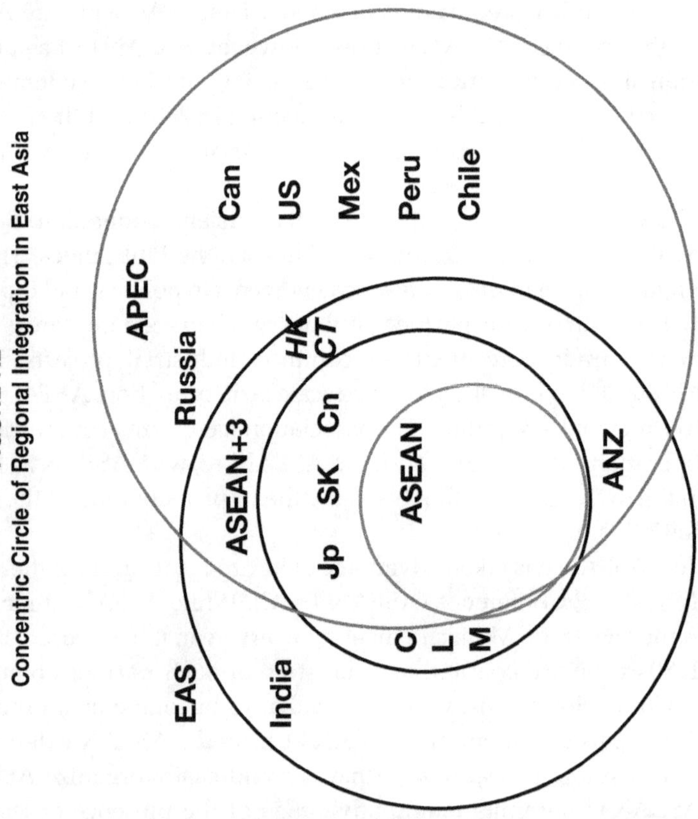

FIGURE 7.2
Concentric Circle of Regional Integration in East Asia

preventing pandemics, environmental protection, and energy cooperation. APEC is referred to as an outer-circle organization for cooperation, but not assigned a major role for East Asian cooperation. It cannot be denied that underlying this paradigm shift is a preference for China and Malaysia against U.S. influence.

Although sitting in the driver's seat of ASEAN+3 and the EAS, ASEAN perceives well the fact that ASEAN is the weakest member of these groupings and has moved to strengthen its economies. At the ASEAN Summit in December 2007, it adopted the ASEAN Charter and all ten leaders signed it. The charter has institutionalized ASEAN as an international organization and announced its plan to build an economic community, political and security community, and social and cultural community by 2015. The blueprint for the economic community details concrete measures to be implemented before 2015. It reflects increased momentum among advanced ASEAN members towards further institutionalization, but some concerns have been made that the blueprint will not be implemented on schedule. Nevertheless, ratification was completed and the charter went into effect at the ASEAN Summit in Bangkok in March 2009.

Solid Economic Vision versus Weak Political and Security Basis

An economic community is at the core of the East Asian Community. Let us confirm its concept here. In July 2003, I, as President of the Institute of Developing Economies/JETRO, invited a representative research institute from each ASEAN member country and organized a Japan-ASEAN Think Tank Meeting in order to conduct a joint study assisting the negotiation for the Japan-ASEAN Comprehensive Economic Partnership (JACEP) Agreement (IDE/JETRO 2003). We explained the basic concept of the JACEP as follows. It is essential to achieve market integration and gains from greater economy rather than merely the reduction of tariffs.

- While Japan-ASEAN (especially its advanced members') economic relations have continued for over thirty years, they have consisted mainly of bilateral relationships between Japan and individual ASEAN members, based on the fragmented individual home markets. Tariff reduction cannot provide a significant impact on a bilateral relationship. By achieving an integrated ASEAN market through which both intermediate parts and finished products move freely, we can accomplish ASEAN-wide business. Some Japanese auto and electronic manufacturers have already started to switch their procurement systems to the integrated ASEAN market.

- Individual ASEAN member governments have to change from domestic protection to competitive policies towards a single ASEAN market. It requires not only reduction of tariffs and non-tariff measures, but also the liberalization of services and investment as well as such facilitation measures as customs procedures, standards, and conformance so that an efficient and seamless business environment may be realized.
- Japan should help ASEAN to accomplish its economic integration so that Japanese firms can do business better. Japan participates in ASEAN's efforts to strengthen capital and financial markets and provides development assistance to latecomer members.

The same concept is applied to East Asia as a whole. The East Asian Community will enable businesses to form regional production networks and utilize them effectively, so that Asian firms become competitive and survive the global competition. JACEP will assist Asian firms institutionally that have already moved in this direction. Incidentally, Japan's Ministry of Economy, Trade and Industry (METI)'s 2007 White Paper states clearly that Japan should promote JACEP for this purpose (METI 2007).

China enjoys the merit of attracting foreign capital and technology with its huge domestic market and seems to be less eager to attempt further integration with neighbouring economies. Nevertheless, further expansion of her domestic market will provide greater business opportunities for Chinese firms. China has already achieved a high level of commodity export and investment dependence, 35.2 per cent and 6.6 per cent respectively (Appendix Table 6). The ASEAN-China FTA was not only motivated by the political soothing of her neighbours, but also by the expansion of Chinese products into the neighbouring markets. The momentum towards the East Asian Community is inexorable.

However, it will be difficult to achieve an East Asian political and security community any time soon. Any regional integration is pursued for both peace and prosperity. The political and security basis is far less mature in East Asia than in Europe.

Let us compare briefly the participation in regional integration by European countries — Germany, France, or Italy — with that of Japan.

Territorial struggle and war continued between national sovereign states in Europe from the seventeenth to the first half of the twentieth century. National borders were redrawn many times to the extent that many people speak a neighbouring country's language as their native tongue. After World War II Europeans were weary of war and pan-Europeanism spread so that they preferred to lower national borders rather than to redraw them. Regional integration was attempted in Western Europe in the form of the European Economic Community and the European Free Trade Association in the 1950s. It continued during the Cold War under the support of the United States. It has succeeded in achieving prosperity through the Single Market (1992) and European Union (1998), expanding its membership to twenty-seven members, including those in Eastern Europe after the end of the Cold War (1989). Some member states must have paid economic costs in assisting the development of other members, but no strong voice has been heard against the regional economic integration or for reverting the process. The countries have enjoyed peace without territorial struggles or military conflict between themselves for the past sixty years.

On the other hand, the history of East Asia has been quite different. Japan, Korea, and China adopted their isolation policies until the second half of the nineteenth century saw colonial wars and imperial aggression for a century. The Korean War and Vietnam War occurred after World War II, and severe conflicts remained between capitalistic market economies and state-planned socialist economies during the Cold War. Only with the open economy policy by China in the 1980s and by Vietnam in the 1990s have trade and investment flourished and the market mechanism introduced to the socialist regimes. However, North Korea still remains isolated and its military threat continues. The people of East Asia do not yet share the like-mindedness for ending struggles and conflicts as evidenced in Europe.

A series of recent conflicts remind us of the absence of such like-mindedness in East Asia. Conflicts between China and Japan near the Spratly Islands immediately triggered anti-Japanese demonstrations in a number of Chinese cities and harassment of Chinese Embassy staff in Tokyo. The recent proliferation of Chinese warships in the Eastern Pacific has caused serious concern among neighbouring countries. The announcement of Kim Chong Won as the successor of his father in North Korea, the Chinese Government's quick support of this, and the Chinese Government's imprisonment of the Chinese laureate of the 2010 Nobel

Peace Prize remind us of clear differences in their political regime from our democratic ones.

We expect that these differences in political regime will be mitigated in the long term by the mutual efforts of both sides. China will introduce democratic and rule-based elements into their political regime as her economy develops and living standards rises. The economic merits mentioned above will support and strengthen the convergence process. Nevertheless, regional economic integration in East Asia is currently constrained by these weak political and security bases.

Necessity for China-Japan-South Korea Trilateral Cooperation

China, Japan, and South Korea have been nearest neighbours for the past two thousand years. But Japan's aggression to its neighbours in the first half of the last century as well as the political and economic impacts of the Cold War in the 1950–70s impeded closer contacts and delayed the formation of close cooperation networks. Japan started formal diplomatic relations with South Korea in 1965. South Korea has now become Japan's fourth-largest trading partner, with frequent movement of people in business, tourism, and education. Japan established formal diplomatic relations with China in 1979 to the extent that China has become the country's largest partner, both in terms of commodity trade and foreign direct investment (FDI).

However, bilateral FTAs have not been concluded yet between any of the three countries. Regarding plans for an FTA between Japan and South Korea, a joint study was conducted as early as 1999, immediately after the monumental visit to Japan by South Korean President Kim Dae Jung in 1998. This was upgraded to a tripartite consultation by business people, academics, and officials of the two countries, and formal negotiations began in 2003. These have been however suspended since 2004. Potential mutual benefit from a bilateral FTA between the two neighbours is well perceived. But South Korea's concern about the long-running trade deficit, fears of dominance by Japanese businesses, and reluctance regarding technology transfers on the part of Japanese businesses are often cited as major impediments to a final conclusion (Yamazawa 2000). In contrast, South Korea signed an FTA with the United States in 2007 and with the European Union in 2010.

A joint study on a proposed FTA between China and South Korea was initiated by the Development Research Center of China's State Department and the Korean Institute of International Economic Policy (KIEP) in 2004. This was upgraded to a tripartite joint study by industry, academia, and government in 2006, but no official negotiation has been initiated yet. China has taken an active stance. On the other hand, whilst South Korea recognizes the great potential merits of an FTA with its largest export market and investment destination, such industries as steel, general machinery, and chemicals feel threatened by the rapid catch-up growth of Chinese industries and products.

A potential China-Japan FTA is the most delayed, with no move witnessed yet. Both economies have both positive and negative aspects, and neither has yet taken any initiative in this regard.

Instead of searching for a balance between the three pairs, it is possible that they could jump into a trilateral investment treaty from the beginning. The C-J-ROK (China-Japan-Republic of Korea) Trilateral Summit started on the occasion of ASEAN-related summit meetings in 1999, taking advantage of the presence of the three leaders. With President Kim Dae Jung's proposal in 2001, a joint study of a trilateral FTA was initiated by the Development Research Center of China's State Department, Japan's National Institute for Research Advancement, and the Korean Institute of International Economic Policy (KIEP), all being government-related think tanks. They jointly conducted questionnaire surveys administered to businessmen in the three countries, jointly organized open seminars in the individual countries, and issued a joint report at the end of 2008 (*C-J-ROK Joint Report* 2008). The report stressed a clear benefit from closer cooperation among the three countries and that 70 to 80 per cent of businessmen in each country supported the trilateral FTA, but added that each country is constrained by adjustment costs in sensitive sectors. The report concludes with a suggestion that the joint study and public relations activities should be continued in order to maintain the momentum for closer trilateral cooperation.

On 13 December 2008 the Trilateral Summit was organized in Fukuoka, Japan independently from the ASEAN Summit so that the three leaders, Chinese Prime Minister Wen Jiabao, Japanese Prime Minister Taro Aso, and South Korean President Lee Myung-Bak, could have more time for discussion on trilateral issues. However, it is never easy to form a joint initiative among the three. It is well-known that such initiatives have been prevented by historical legacies and diplomatic rivalry, and that the difference in economic system between Japan, South Korea, and China sets a high barrier for negotiating an FTA. The three leaders started with easy issues at the trilateral table, leaving difficult ones to individual pairs of bilateral talks, and issued the joint statements emphasizing strengthening trilateral cooperation in international finance, improving the business environment, and announced their action plans (C-J-ROK Trilateral Summit 2008).

On 10 October 2009 the Second Trilateral Summit was hosted by Prime Minister Wen Jaibao in Beijing, after Prime Minister Yukio Hatoyama replaced Mr Aso. They confirmed the joint declarations from the previous Trilateral Summit and issued two joint statements. First, they acknowledged the achievements over the past ten years of deepening mutually beneficial cooperation in various economic areas. Second, they reviewed and reaffirmed their cooperation on sustainable development, referring to water-resources, forest management, clean energy and energy efficiency, and successful achievement of the Copenhagen Conference (C-J-ROK Trilateral Joint Statement, 2009). Later, on the occasion of the ASEAN and Related Summits on 25 October, Economic and Trade Ministers of the three countries acknowledged their follow-up activities for the Business Environment Action Agenda, and expanded the joint study on the trilateral FTA to include businesses people and government officials.

Investment policy has been assigned a strategic priority in the trilateral cooperation. FDI has become instrumental for further strengthening the economic partnership among the three and they have agreed to reach a substantive agreement on a Trilateral Investment Treaty. As a matter of fact, the three governments have been conducting joint studies and consulting on the legal framework since 2004, and began negotiations for a trilateral investment treaty, one step before FTA, in 2007. The economic and trade ministers agreed to conclude the Trilateral Investment Treaty negotiations in early 2010.

Investment treaties have been concluded in increasing numbers in the global trend towards regionalism. They used to focus on the protection of foreign investors in most favoured nations (MFN), national treatment, fair treatment, free fund movement, limitation and guarantee against expropriation, transparency of legal and administrative procedures, and dispute mediation and settlement processes with host governments, which are *post-measures* after investment is admitted. But they have tended to include *pre-measures* in providing MFN and national treatment, transparency of prohibition for foreign investment, and limitation of performance requirements, which have the element of *investment liberalization*.

Japan and South Korea are latecomers in negotiating investment treaties, but have concluded ones with both post- and pre-measures. China has increased the number of investment treaties recently, with perfect provisions for post-measures but is cautious about pre-measures. Investment protection is necessary in order to invite FDI, but China apparently wishes to keep policy intervention in upgrading FDI with further technological transfer. China conceded some liberalization along trade related investment measures (TRIM) at its accession to the World Trade Organization (WTO) in 2001. But the existing investment treaty between Japan and China admits various exceptions and performance requirements. South Korea's new investment treaty with China does not include pre-national-treatment, but restricts performance requirements in only four aspects of TRIM. It is likely for the three governments to conclude their negotiations with some additional liberalization of pre-measures by China.

There are a large variety of areas for possible mutual benefit from closer cooperation among the three countries, as mentioned in the joint leaders' statements. Political will and initiative by the three leaders is also vital in promoting cooperation in Northeast Asia, i.e., China's three northeastern provinces, Japan, South Korea, North Korea, Mongolia, and the Russian Far East. These countries and regions are endowed with different natural and human resources and have the potential to benefit greatly from an international division of labour, which has been left out of emerging regionalism in Asia. This is due in part to the lingering legacy of the Cold War, while North Korea remains isolated and there is ongoing tension in regard to security. However, it cannot be denied that the different economic systems of the countries and regions concerned have also hindered effective cooperation.

Nevertheless, we have seen moves aimed at alleviating political and security tensions, such as the resolution of the Eastern Border dispute between China and Russia, North-South talks on the Korean Peninsula, efforts to normalize diplomatic relations between Japan and Russia, and the Japan–North Korea Pyongyang Declaration. At the same time, the dynamic development of China's three northeastern provinces, which are located at the heart of this sub-region, has provided momentum for greater economic dynamism involving South Korea, Japan, and Russia as well. The United Nations Development Programme's Tumen River Area

Development Programme and a few track-two approaches have been undertaken to facilitate the development of this sub-region over the past two decades (Yamazawa et al. 2007).

Many expect that the three economies will strengthen their trilateral ties, but it is also a fact that this cannot be done quickly so long as each pursues its own national interest, because each differs in its expectations of the others. Besides, there is a weak political and security basis underlying relations between the three nations. They need to emphasize greater mutual benefit from trilateral cooperation.

Neither Hong Kong nor Chinese Taipei have been mentioned in the FTA moves in East Asia, although both are included in Figure 2. Outsiders are hesitant to refer to them because of the delicate political relationship between the three economies. However, a big change has been occurring here together with the rise of the Chinese economy. As we saw in Chapter 2, China's trade and investment have expanded immensely with all partners and has been a powerful engine driving the world economy. We have also seen that Hong Kong and Chinese Taipei have participated in this. It is well known that businesses from the two economies have invested in China, provided technology and marketing know-how, and contributed greatly to the rise of China through their Chinese subsidiaries. Institutional arrangements have also been developed. China concluded the Closer Economic Relations Agreement with Hong Kong in 2002 and the Economic Cooperation Framework Agreement with Chinese Taipei in June 2010, under which commodities, funds, and personnel have moved freely across borders. The two agreements have institutionalized the Greater Chinese economy. We may assume that Hong Kong and Chinese Taipei will go together with China in the China-Japan-Republic of Korea FTA, EAFTA (East Asia Free Trade Area), or CEPEA (Comprehensive Economic Partnership for East Asia).

The United States' Engagement in Asia

The United States has had close economic relations with East Asia for the past decades. Japan, South Korea, Chinese Taipei, Hong Kong, and ASEAN members used to earn a large part of their foreign exchange from exports to the large U.S. market during their initial stages of industrialization following World War II, and China and Vietnam have followed suit for the past two decades. East Asia has become a major market for American products and services as well as a major investment destination. On the other hand the United States had established security alliances with several Asian countries during the Cold War which continue to be important to her global strategy.

Thus the United States is concerned about her economic interests being impeded by any developments in East Asia. Since the 1960s American businessmen and economists have participated in Pacific economic cooperation activities, and since 1989 the U.S. Government has participated in APEC as a founding member (Chapter 2). When Malaysian Prime Minister Mahathir proposed an East Asian Economic Caucus (EAEC) in 1990, U.S. Secretary of State Baker fiercely objected to it and managed to have it aborted. Although any severe objection such as this has not been expressed recently, the United States is still intensely watching developments in East Asia. The U.S. business sector in particular is watching East Asia closesly. On the other hand, East Asian nations for their part differ in how to respond to U.S. interests. It is not clear yet how ASEAN+3 and EAS members will manage their relations with outside economies, the United States, Canada, and Latin American economies on the Pacific coast.

The United States has traditionally believed in the market economy and promoted liberalization in trade and investment. Partly because of her propensity for excessive consumption at home, she has accumulated a huge trade deficit over the past thirty years, especially with emerging economies in East Asia. Thus the strong demand for market openings and export expansion to East Asia are high priorities of her trade policy agenda. When it hosted APEC in 1993 the United States proposed in the first leaders' declaration that APEC should achieve "free and open trade in the region" (Chapter 2).

In 2006 the APEC Business Advisory Council proposed to APEC leaders a Free Trade Area of the Asia-Pacific (FTAAP) based on the suggestion of the American council member. In spite of a prudent attitude on the Asian side, the FTAAP was adopted as a long-term agenda of APEC in 2007 (APEC/LM 2007). President Obama stressed the expansion of American exports to East Asia as a major policy tool for increasing employment at home (USTR 2011).

The United States has further enhanced her engagement in East Asia over the past years. In December 2008, after the Lehman shock and spread of global depression, the Office of the United States Trade Representative (USTR) expressed U.S. interest in joining the Trans-Pacific Partnership (TPP). In October 2009 Assistant Secretary Kurt Campbell testified before the House Committee on Foreign Affairs Subcommittee on Asia, the Pacific, and the Global Environment. He described the strategic framework for U.S. engagement, referred to not only economic but also "broader security challenges" such as climate change, the proliferation of weapons of mass destruction, extremist groups in Southeast Asia, unresolved territorial disputes, growing competition over energy and natural resources, greenhouse gas emissions, and natural disasters, and stressed that their resolution requires U.S. cooperation and leadership (USTR 2009). The USTR report (2010) indicated the importance of its economic relationship with APEC economies in quantitative terms and referred to APEC as an instrument to promote regional and global trade and investment liberalization. The 2011 report reiterates that the U.S. host achieved "a robust agenda leading to practical, concrete, and ambitious outcomes on the foundation provided by the preceding Japanese host last year" (USTR 2011, p. 137).

These moves by the U.S. Government were preceded by intense discussion on how to manage her relationship with the rising Chinese economy. The United States characterizes her relationship with China as a "strategic partner". She has welcomed the conversion of China to a market economy since the late 1980s and her trade and investment with China has expanded five-fold so that China has become the States' largest trade and investment partner outside of North America. She supported China's accession to the WTO in 2001 and perceives that the environment of the international economy has helped the rise of the Chinese economy over the past decade. The United States expects that China will behave as a responsible stakeholder in the global economic regime (U.S.-China Summit Statement 2011; Geithner 2011).

On the other hand, concern exists over the military expansion and security risk of China, and some insist that the United States must hedge against China's rise (Zoelick 2006). The U.S. strategy for regional cooperation in the Asia Pacific is affected by all these considerations (Nye and Armitage Report 2007). Several East Asian economies have accepted enhanced American economic engagement in Asia so as to ensure American involvement in the security of the Asia Pacific.

A Road Map for Asia Pacific Integration

The Asia Pacific has been the most dynamic region and has played the driving role of the world economy. Unlike in Europe, the institutionalization of regional economic cooperation has been delayed and the region still faces big challenges in diplomacy and security as elaborated earlier.

However, in order to realize its growth potential, it is essential to intelligently promote its institutionalization.

What will be its likely road map? Will the move for the East Asian Community go ahead, or will the trans-Pacific move for FTAAP prevail? APEC 2010 in Yokohama identified ASEAN+3, the EAS, and TPP as road maps to FTAAP to be promoted in parallel. The ASEAN+3, EAS, and APEC/TPP have different but partly overlapping memberships and action agendas. Let us analyze them in detail and indicate challenges that need to be overcome for each of the road maps.

ASEAN+3 has a solid base for building an economic community to allow East Asia to survive global competition, but it faces various impediments existing among its members. Their current achievement to date remains only the Chiang Mai Initiative for currency exchanges among the thirteen members. Regarding its further expansion, ASEAN has already concluded six sets of ASEAN+1 type FTA/EPAs, but does not seem to be moving any time soon to merge them towards ASEAN+3 or ASEAN+6. It is partly because they are satisfied with the status quo and partly because they will be heavily engaged in the ASEAN Economic Community process for the next decade. However, much delay will reduce the momentum towards the East Asian Community. Thus the merging process needs to be pushed by China, Japan, and South Korea, as well as part of their trilateral cooperation. But, as we saw earlier in this chapter, trilateral cooperation will not proceed as fast as desired.

EAS started as a luncheon meeting at the ASEAN PMC in 2005 and its membership consists of ASEAN+6. It has been discussing such issues for broader regional cooperation as antiterrorism, natural disasters, and climate change. At the 2009 APEC in Singapore, President Obama expressed the U.S. interest in joining EAS and the United States signed the ASEAN Treaty of Amity, which is a prerequisite for making an agreement with ASEAN. In October 2010, the EAS in Hanoi agreed to invite both the United States and Russia to the 2011 EAS, and U.S. Secretary of State Hillary Clinton and Russian Foreign Minister Ruslov attended the EAS/FM. EAS will become ASEAN+8 and the overlap of membership with APEC will be further strengthened.

EAS will continue to discuss broader regional cooperation but it will also pick up some security issues, taking advantage of the participation of the United States and Russia. The EAS Defence Ministers' meeting was held in Shanghai in early October where agreement was reached on a principle of non-recourse to military power in the event of a conflict.

Regional economic integration is inevitably constrained by the political and security dimensions of the region. Because of this constraint APEC has confined itself to economic issues. It is only at the Leaders' Meetings that they have started to occasionally discuss political and security issues such as antiterrorism, taking advantage of the presence of the leaders of the major powers in the region. If EAS can serve the political and security dimension it will support the development of APEC to a more institutionalized regional economic integration.

Both ASEAN+3 and EAS have published their own FTA concepts, the EAFTA and CEPEA respectively, which, however, have remained as study reports without any concrete action plans (East Asian Vision Group 2001; East Asian Summit 2006).

On the other hand, **APEC** has twenty years' experiences in trade and investment facilitation such as streamlining customs procedures, disseminating information technology, harmonizing standards and certification schemes, and promptly issuing business visas. Industrialized economies have transferred technology to help developing economies build their capacity in these areas so that steady progress has been made towards the Bogor Goals. It seems that ASEAN members have benefited from their APEC affiliation in implementing their facilitation measures within the ASEAN Economic Community blueprint

TPP has currently been negotiated among nine APEC economies. Although generated from the APEC process, it will be a binding agreement with a high-level FTA. The United States has taken the initiative in its discussions on its FTA components and plans to conclude them in time for the Honolulu APEC in October 2011.

It will take some time to finalize a regional economic institution in the Asia Pacific. That is, we need not decide immediately to adopt one option and discard others. ASEAN+3, EAS, and TPP may be floated in the next decade or so, in the sense that each of the three continues to be partially implemented when its own specialized area meets an immediate need, but none can be completed due to various constraints. As each proceeds with partly overlapping members in parallel, each will interact with others and necessary modification will be made in membership and agendas when a conflict arises.

Each has an annual conference series and its activity is expanded with a "proponent-driven" modality in which a cooperation project is proposed by a member with a real resource input which is adopted so long as other members see it as beneficial. If China and Japan increase trade and investment liberalization beyond the Chiang Mai Initiative, ASEAN+3 will proceed further. The expansion of the EAS to include the United States and Russia in 2011 will strengthen broader regional cooperation, which, we expect, will also improve the political and security basis of the Asia-Pacific. APEC has moved towards the post-Bogor agenda in 2010, and continued the TILF process and activated the TPP channel towards FTAAP, which will inevitably affect the ASEAN+3 and EAS processes. Rivalry will push the three ahead through interaction. This interaction will continue for at least a decade during which the Asia-Pacific regional institution will evolve with better coordination among participating economies. This will be a likely road map for regional integration of a wider East Asia and the Pacific.

Here we witness two moves towards regional economic cooperation: ASEAN+3 and TPP. ASEAN+3, spured by China, excludes the United States, while the TPP negotiated under U.S. leadership does not include China. The joint U.S.-China leaders' statement in January 2011 welcomed China as a responsible stakeholder, but the Chinese feel that she is excluded. Japanese Prime Minister Kan has taken a strong initiative in joining TPP, but the current TPP composition (excluding China) does not promise great merit. In order to mitigate the conflict between the two moves, we need to strengthen APEC's continued TILF process as an effective incubator for the FTAAP, as was committed by APEC leaders in Yokohama last November (Chapter 4). The United States hosts APEC this year and takes its leadership throughout the year. Japan, as the preceding host, should help the United States in clarifying their strong commitment to the Bogor Goals and FTAAP.

Note

1. However, this move has made no headway for several years.

Appendix

Appendix Table 1: Trade Matrix of APEC Economies: 1995, 2001, 2007 (million U.S. dollars)

Source: Jointly produced by Ippei Yamazawa and Chiang Chunhua in May 2010. Original figures for 2001 and 2007 are compiled from the Institute of Trade and Investment, *ITI's International Trade Matrix by Commodity: 2009*. The 1995 figures are compiled from the United Nations, Direction of Trade, on an export basis, supplemented by the country statistics of Chinese Taipei. ITI compiled its trade matrix based on all available trade statistics of individual countries on a fob basis. The total world trade of ITI's Trade Matrix amounts to 97.9 per cent of that of the IMF's International Financial Statistics.

Notes

1. Economies are listed not in alphabetical order, but by geographical proximity, focusing on East Asia so that it provides us with a clear view of the trade pattern in the Asia Pacific.
2. In the trade matrix, 0 stands for 0 and — stands for no figure in the original statistics, while an empty cell shows no trade as in the case of intraregional trade for a single economy. They are all treated as 0 in summation.
3. World total trade represents the sum of all reporting countries' exports to the world.

EXPORT FROM	IMPORT TO	Japan	China	Hong Kong	South Korea	Ch.Taipei	Brunei	Indonesia	Malaysia	The Philippines	Singapore	Thailand	Vietnam	Australia	New Zealand	PNG	USA	Canada	Chile	Mexico	Peru	Russia	APEC(21)	EU(15)	WORLD
JP	1995		21,934	27,780	31,292	28,984	131	9,969	16,802	7,100	23,006	19,719	922	8,104	1,626	121	122,034	5,828	916	3,572	300	1,170	331,310	70,367	443,116
	2001		30,941	23,249	25,286	24,214	56	6,403	11,013	8,190	14,714	11,873	1,776	7,683	1,181	47	121,153	6,564	468	4,088	276	715	299,890	64,351	403,247
	2007		109,279	38,895	54,305	44,863	123	9,065	15,048	9,478	21,827	25,603	5,685	14,226	2,494	152	143,664	10,541	1,584	10,250	549	10,763	528,397	96,524	714,126
CN	1995	28,466		36,003	6,688	3,095	34	1,438	1,281	1,030	3,500	1,752	722	1,626	232	16	24,744	1,533	411	195	146	1,674	114,586	19,258	148,797
	2001	45,078		46,503	12,544	5,006	17	2,847	3,223	1,622	5,795	2,504	1,805	3,574	435	19	54,319	3,350	816	1,802	177	2,715	194,152	40,965	266,661
	2007	102,116		184,289	56,129	23,480	113	12,609	17,702	7,505	29,680	11,979	11,906	17,998	2,161	213	232,761	19,363	4,416	11,707	1,678	28,484	776,287	221,345	1,218,155
HK	1995	10,596	57,861		2,804	4,619	24	1,062	1,547	2,009	4,944	1,615	637	2,393	328	30	37,851	2,633	617	392	3	315	132,280	25,959	173,750
	2001	11,261	70,407		3,430	4,642	51	843	1,635	1,925	3,852	1,899	543	2,258	276	9	42,327	2,933	413	1,159	54	212	150,127	27,547	191,244
	2007	15,357	168,683		7,265	7,134	30	1,815	3,249	2,866	6,511	3,803	2,448	4,445	521	10	47,300	3,440	400	1,601	117	900	277,894	44,584	349,663
SK	1995	17,088	9,192	10,646		3,887	—	2,962	2,957	1,494	6,700	2,428	1,355	1,570	—	—	24,173	1,794	637	943	—	1,407	89,233	15,319	125,058
	2001	16,506	18,190	9,452		5,835	16	3,280	2,628	2,535	4,080	1,848	1,732	2,173	272	9	31,211	2,036	573	2,149	188	938	105,651	19,627	150,439
	2007	26,370	81,985	18,654		13,027	27	5,771	5,704	4,420	11,949	4,488	5,760	4,691	699	18	45,766	3,506	3,115	7,482	466	8,088	251,989	43,501	371,489
Ch.Taipei	1995	14,329	14,785	16,710	2,560		24	1,870	3,952	1,537	5,116	3,421	515	2,993	361	8	30,158	2,035	202	716	68	88	101,448	19,612	121,308
	2001	12,714	4,727	26,858	3,264		11	1,469	3,050	2,141	4,037	2,118	1,720	1,358	194	7	27,552	1,558	176	1,016	88	261	94,320	18,302	122,409
	2007	15,136	58,430	34,188	7,475		17	2,886	5,250	4,779	10,048	5,064	6,719	3,184	543	9	31,025	1,816	281	1,491	201	796	189,337	23,287	234,710
BR	1995	1,220	—	1	—	46		1	4	7	203	263	—	16	—	—	36	3		—	3	—	1,803	187	2,108
	2001	1,527	133	1	370	0		33	5	0	163	348	0	205	20	—	399	2		0	0	0	3,208	25	3,233
	2007	2,259	217	1	841	0		1,678	86	0	126	108	—	947	134	—	405	2		0	0	0	6,806	50	7,078
ID	1995	12,348	1,761	1,601	2,924	1,813	40		1,010	550	2,727	671	332	951	132	23	6,476	376	101	104	12	14	36,130	7,344	48,665
	2001	13,010	2,201	1,290	3,772	2,188	22		1,779	815	5,364	1,064	322	1,845	145	28	7,749	390	85	230	21	62	42,382	7,745	56,321
	2007	23,633	9,676	1,687	7,583	2,597	43		5,096	1,854	10,502	3,054	1,355	3,395	362	70	11,614	551	135	361	42	338	83,947	12,744	114,101
ML	1995	9,199	1,889	3,941	2,015	2,280	289	970		651	14,960	2,868	269	1,122	182	37	15,313	602	71	335	—	101	57,094	10,468	74,037
	2001	11,770	3,821	4,063	2,963	3,263	273	1,563		1,287	14,913	3,360	474	2,052	297	28	17,808	547	80	647	13	131	69,353	11,964	88,202
	2007	16,099	15,461	8,150	6,707	4,795	403	5,174		2,550	25,786	8,735	2,331	5,942	755	97	27,513	956	83	1,173	57	630	133,396	21,156	176,311
PH	1995	2,740	209	822	442	568	3	126	314		994	799	124	142	22	3	6,217	196	34	36	4	—	13,795	3,061	17,502
	2001	5,057	793	1,580	1,044	2,127	4	133	1,112		2,308	1,358	62	225	19	2	8,843	282	12	163	10	14	25,283	6,195	32,151
	2007	7,291	5,716	5,802	1,783	1,869	6	522	2,504		3,127	1,403	436	528	114	20	8,540	258	27	160	9	26	40,188	8,353	50,270
SG	1995	9,219	2,759	10,126	3,243	4,813	1,466	—	22,665	1,928		6,824	1,790	2,592	384	172	21,576	572	87	187	21	911	91,335	15,826	118,268
	2001	9,331	5,326	10,814	4,684	6,260	410	2,832	21,107	3,083		5,295	2,103	3,153	402	193	18,728	402	35	736	14	133	95,040	16,252	121,691
	2007	14,392	28,924	31,346	10,610	9,151	696	29,471	38,612	6,131		12,388	6,515	11,194	1,559	314	26,205	1,986	88	1,089	25	500	231,197	29,757	299,404
TH	1995	9,477	1,642	2,921	801	1,354	64	811	1,554	414	7,917		468	777	93	21	10,078	613	47	53	21		39,126	8,515	56,467
	2001	9,942	2,850	3,284	1,226	1,908	37	1,360	2,713	1,152	5,263		794	1,355	182	15	13,193	782	64	426	13	81	46,641	10,476	64,909
	2007	19,290	15,918	9,194	3,178	3,551	98	5,101	8,353	3,108	10,219		4,082	6,136	656	65	20,596	1,456	342	914	124	614	112,995	20,891	163,119
VN	1995	1,560	302	158	—	246	—	84	114	39	408	39		213	8	—	191	56	—	—	11	35	3,464	1,374	5,723
	2001	2,510	1,417	317	406	426	1	264	337	368	1,044	323		1,042	18	3	1,066	107	9	44	2	194	9,900	3,004	15,029
	2007	6,090	3,646	583	1,243	1,042	—	1,153	1,555	965	2,234	1,030		3,802	67	15	10,111	539	47	360	16	458	34,958	8,518	48,561
AU	1995	12,184	2,293	2,090	4,474	2,422	47	1,737	1,634	739	2,831	1,270	152		3,833	673	3,358	882	105	57	14	109	40,904	5,865	52,692
	2001	12,246	3,904	2,162	4,925	2,777	24	1,660	1,338	682	2,768	1,183	257		3,705	534	6,140	937	71	209	31	95	45,649	7,605	63,233
	2007	26,790	20,006	2,358	11,301	4,986	26	3,281	2,642	928	3,417	3,704	1,196		7,968	1,388	8,441	1,501	168	554	70	555	101,280	15,825	141,379
NZ	1995	2,225	347	418	707	398	11	199	287	137	192	184	39	2,785		50	1,361	224	59	73	59	113	9,868	1,936	13,738
	2001	1,715	565	330	605	298	1	231	293	237	168	173	156	2,594		41	2,037	265	21	225	36	14	10,004	2,055	13,714
	2007	2,475	1,440	431	977	568	2	575	481	494	509	418	268	5,929		88	3,102	397	40	444	25	115	18,778	3,793	26,958
PNG	1995	664	71	39	204	8	—	6	24	80	26	21	1	867	47		49	1	—	—	—	—	2,108	507	2,644
	2001	268	110	6	78	11	—	11	8	59	20	63	1	644	36		39	5	—	0	—	0	1,360	235	1,599
	2007	743	422	15	124	10	—	13	34	106	23	80	21	2,144	62		109	3	—	0	0	3	3,910	563	4,659
US	1995	64,298	11,749	14,220	25,413	19,295	190	3,395	8,818	5,294	15,318	6,402	253	10,788	1,693	51		126,024	3,613	46,312	1,775	3,066	367,967	123,615	584,743
	2001	57,452	19,182	14,028	22,181	18,122	104	2,521	9,358	7,660	17,652	5,989	460	10,931	2,111	22		163,424	3,118	101,296	1,564	2,716	459,890	158,767	729,100
	2007	62,703	65,236	20,118	34,645	26,309	140	4,235	11,680	7,712	26,284	8,455	1,903	19,212	2,814	66		248,888	8,315	136,092	4,120	7,365	696,292	237,884	1,162,479
CA	1995	8,531	2,293	1,221	1,943	1,224	3	438	398	224	345	382	24	776	127	3	152,896		276	786	103	128	172,121	11,282	192,197
	2001	5,388	2,747	802	1,302	659	1	302	222	225	254	286	38	697	140	2	227,260		238	1,778	123	187	242,649	11,876	261,046
	2007	8,597	8,908	1,449	2,815	1,438	3	936	557	428	863	553	270	1,638	380	3	332,002		714	4,637	310	1,072	367,573	31,357	420,646
CH	1995	2,906	288	87	897	703	—	158	88	66	79	150	—	60	15	3	2,398	96		132	438	—	3,142	4,449	16,024
	2001	2,167	1,027	49	578	361	—	42	32	56	24	46	4	41	9	0	3,216	268		832	480	17	9,251	4,607	17,616
	2007	7,092	9,950	101	3,849	1,749	—	237	73	315	113	293	108	279	26	0	8,420	1,201		2,368	1,034	228	37,434	15,418	65,788
MX	1995	928	37	—	89	44	—	16	27	6	173	31	—	56	4	—	66,475	1,979	490		179	—	70,534	3,389	48,430
	2001	621	282	120	293	172	0	14	67	16	242	63	3	88	19	—	140,296	3,070	374		173	18	145,931	5,333	158,443
	2007	1,913	1,895	328	680	272	0	43	123	75	336	167	39	561	33	5	223,202	6,491	1,170		677	160	238,169	14,048	271,958
PE	1995	501	355	50	159	200	—	25	70	42	2	23	2	11	1	—	956	140	153	96		19	1,376	1,661	5,575
	2001	380	426	21	111	86	—	39	15	20	8	70	9	36	2	0	1,695	143	282	128		32	3,505	1,806	6,850
	2007	2,184	3,041	71	883	395	—	26	4	9	4	46	48	98	11	0	5,250	1,785	1,693	269		14	15,831	4,690	27,588
RU	1995	3,173	3,377	311	747	463	—	81	573	124	490	392	322	29	2	—	5,092	121	22	28	32		15,379	26,051	81,096
	2001	2,428	3,955	113	827	262	—	29	259	45	709	69	157	10	7	0	2,858	47	20	94	34		11,922	24,729	68,416
	2007	7,403	15,031	245	6,056	885	—	250	440	117	922	326	462	47	5	0	7,067	313	22	285	182		40,062	115,248	279,724
APEC(21)	1995	211,652	133,144	129,145	87,402	76,462	2,326	25,348	64,119	23,471	89,931	49,254	7,927	37,871	9,090	1,211	531,432	145,708	7,841	54,017	3,189	9,150	1,701,854	376,045	2,331,938
	2001	221,372	173,006	145,040	89,890	78,616	1,028	25,876	60,193	32,120	83,377	39,932	12,417	41,964	9,470	961	727,888	187,111	6,859	117,021	3,298	8,535	2,065,548	443,464	2,835,553
	2007	367,933	623,863	357,905	218,450	148,122	1,726	84,842	119,192	53,839	164,482	91,699	51,553	106,395	21,365	2,532	1,193,092	304,994	22,640	181,237	9,703	61,110	4,185,634	969,536	6,148,166
EU(15)	1995	48,870	21,313	20,732	18,099	13,713	773	7,989	11,820	3,027	16,577	11,202	—	14,595	2,969	68	136,872	16,383	3,156	6,728	1,339	18,003	374,228	1,385,800	2,351,363
	2001	39,826	27,243	19,260	13,874	11,560	—	3,986	8,429	4,058	13,489	6,642	1,649	13,881	2,068	—	218,122	19,864	3,293	13,764	898	27,688	449,594	1,429,616	2,466,883
	2007	56,651	93,929	27,657	32,416	17,496	1,793	7,101	14,931	5,211	26,699	10,337	4,649	31,705	3,814	83	345,041	33,767	6,266	27,639	2,079	100,657	849,919	2,844,826	4,801,884
WORLD	1995	335,882	129,113	192,751	135,119	93,193	3,513	40,630	77,751	28,337	124,507	70,786	11,803	57,418	13,958	1,262	770,852	163,925	15,914	44,893	7,687	60,945	2,380,239	2,012,120	5,078,010
	2001	315,571	221,052	174,791	130,350	101,682	1,186	34,636	73,096	39,820	109,697	56,136	16,827	60,140	12,551	994	1,089,024	216,926	15,407	136,986	5,887	48,171	2,860,931	2,291,204	6,107,443
	2007	563,672	843,361	405,594	327,425	204,451	3,555	103,649	145,316	66,260	230,510	130,500	66,360	150,516	27,628	2,641	1,866,565	369,062	41,262	224,528	18,366	222,945	6,014,166	4,865,324	13,636,373

Appendix Table 2: Consolidated Trade Matrix of APEC Economies: 1995, 2001, 2007 (million U.S. dollars)

Notes: Economies are grouped as follows:

East Asia 3:	South Korea, Hong Kong, Chinese Taipei
ASEAN 7:	Brunei, Indonesia, Malaysia, the Philippines, Singapore, Thailand, Vietnam
Oceania 3:	Australia, New Zealand, Papua New Guinea
America 4:	Canada, Chile, Mexico, Peru

Source: Consolidated from Appendix Table 1.

Appendix Table 2
Consolidated Trade Matrix of APEC Economies: 1995, 2001, 2007 (million US$)

EXPORT FROM	IMPORT TO	Japan	China	East Asia 3	ASEAN 7	Oceania 3	USA	America 4	Russia	APEC(21)	EU(15)	World Total
Japan	1995		21,934	88,056	77,649	9,851	122,034	10,616	1,170	331,310	70,367	443,116
	2001		30,941	72,749	54,025	8,911	121,153	11,396	715	299,890	64,351	403,247
	2007		109,279	138,063	86,830	16,873	143,664	22,925	10,763	528,397	96,524	714,126
China	1995	28,466		45,786	9,757	1,874	24,744	2,285	1,674	114,586	19,258	148,797
	2001	45,078		64,053	17,814	4,028	54,319	6,145	2,715	194,152	40,965	266,661
	2007	102,116		263,898	91,493	20,371	232,761	37,163	28,484	776,287	221,345	1,218,155
East Asia 3	1995	42,013	81,838	41,226	46,169	7,683	92,182	10,040	1,810	322,961	60,890	420,116
	2001	40,481	93,324	53,480	41,413	6,557	101,089	12,342	1,412	350,098	65,475	464,092
	2007	56,863	309,098	87,744	93,604	14,120	124,091	23,917	9,784	719,220	111,372	955,862
ASEAN 7	1995	45,763	8,562	40,115	74,760	6,890	59,887	3,545	1,061	242,747	46,775	322,770
	2001	53,147	16,541	51,988	85,247	11,231	67,786	5,117	614	291,670	55,660	381,536
	2007	89,055	79,557	111,713	208,593	36,171	104,985	10,801	2,567	643,441	101,469	858,844
Oceania 3	1995	15,073	2,711	10,760	9,617	8,255	4,768	1,474	222	52,880	8,308	69,074
	2001	14,229	4,579	11,192	9,334	7,555	8,216	1,799	109	57,014	9,895	78,546
	2007	30,007	21,867	20,771	18,218	17,579	11,652	3,201	673	123,968	20,181	172,995
USA	1995	64,298	11,749	58,928	39,670	12,532		177,724	3,066	367,967	123,615	584,743
	2001	57,452	19,182	54,330	43,744	13,063		269,403	2,716	459,890	158,767	729,100
	2007	62,703	65,236	81,072	60,409	22,092		397,415	7,365	696,292	237,884	1,162,479
America 4	1995	12,866	2,973	6,617	2,772	1,056	222,725	4,868	147	242,764	20,781	262,226
	2001	8,556	4,482	4,553	2,099	1,034	372,467	7,888	255	401,336	23,622	443,955
	2007	19,786	23,795	14,030	5,670	3,033	568,873	22,349	1,473	659,008	65,513	785,980
Russia	1995	3,173	3,377	1,521	1,982	31	5,092	203		15,379	26,051	81,096
	2001	2,428	3,955	1,202	1,268	17	2,858	195		11,922	24,729	68,416
	2007	7,403	15,031	7,187	2,518	52	7,067	803		40,062	115,248	279,724
APEC(21)	1995	211,652	133,144	293,009	262,376	48,172	531,432	210,755	9,150	1,701,854	376,045	2,331,938
	2001	221,372	173,006	313,546	254,943	52,395	727,888	314,289	8,535	2,065,548	443,464	2,835,553
	2007	367,933	623,863	724,478	567,334	130,292	1,193,092	518,574	61,110	4,185,634	969,536	6,148,166
EU(15)	1995	48,870	21,313	52,544	51,388	17,632	136,872	27,606	18,003	374,228	1,385,800	2,351,363
	2001	39,826	27,243	44,694	38,254	15,949	218,122	37,819	27,688	449,594	1,429,616	2,466,883
	2007	56,651	93,929	77,569	70,720	35,602	345,041	69,750	100,657	849,919	2,844,826	4,801,884
World Total	1995	335,882	129,113	421,063	357,327	72,638	770,852	232,419	60,945	2,380,239	2,012,120	5,078,010
	2001	315,571	221,052	406,823	331,398	73,685	1,089,024	375,207	48,171	2,860,931	2,291,204	6,107,443
	2007	563,672	843,361	937,469	746,151	180,785	1,866,565	653,218	222,945	6,014,166	4,865,324	13,636,373

Appendix Table 3: Increase of Trade Flow between APEC Economies: 1995–2001, 2001–07

Note: The percentage increase of trade between 1995 and 2001 is calculated by (2001 value /1995 value – 1) × 100.
Source: Compiled from Appendix Table 1.

Appendix Table 3
Increase of Trade Flow between APEC Economies (%): 1995–2001, 2001–07

EXPORT FROM	IMPORT TO	Japan	China	Hong Kong	South Korea	Ch. Taipei	Brunei	Indonesia	Malaysia	The Philippines	Singapore	Thailand	Vietnam	Australia	New Zealand	PNG	USA	Canada	Chile	Mexico	Peru	Russia	APEC(21)	EU(15)	WORLD
JP	1995–2001		0.41	–0.16	–0.19	–0.16	–0.58	–0.36	–0.34	0.15	–0.36	–0.40	0.93	–0.05	–0.27	–0.61	–0.01	0.13	–0.49	0.14	–0.08	–0.39	–0.09	–0.09	–0.09
	2001–07		2.53	0.67	1.15	0.85	1.22	0.42	0.37	0.16	0.48	1.16	2.20	0.85	1.11	2.25	0.19	0.61	2.38	1.51	0.99	14.06	0.76	0.50	0.77
CN	1995–2001	0.58		0.29	0.88	0.62	–0.49	0.98	1.52	0.57	0.66	0.43	1.50	1.20	0.88	0.20	1.20	1.19	0.98	8.24	0.21	0.62	0.69	1.13	0.79
	2001–07	1.27		2.96	3.47	3.69	5.55	3.43	4.49	3.63	4.12	3.78	5.59	4.04	3.96	10.10	3.29	4.78	4.41	5.50	8.47	9.49	3.00	4.40	3.57
HK	1995–2001	0.06	0.22		0.22	0.00	1.14	–0.21	0.06	–0.04	–0.22	0.18	–0.15	–0.06	–0.16	–0.70	0.12	0.11	–0.33	1.96	16.89	–0.33	0.13	0.06	0.10
	2001–07	0.36	1.40		1.12	0.54	–0.42	1.15	0.99	0.49	0.69	1.00	3.51	0.97	0.89	0.09	0.12	0.17	–0.03	0.38	1.17	3.24	0.85	0.62	0.83
SK	1995–2001	–0.03	0.98	–0.11		0.50	—	0.11	–0.11	0.70	–0.39	–0.24	0.28	0.38	—	—	0.29	0.13	–0.10	1.28	—	–0.33	0.18	0.28	0.20
	2001–07	0.60	3.51	0.97		1.23	0.62	0.76	1.17	0.74	1.93	1.43	2.33	1.16	1.57	0.98	0.47	0.72	4.44	2.48	1.48	7.62	1.39	1.22	1.47
Ch. Taipei	1995–2001	–0.11	–0.68	0.61	0.27		–0.52	–0.21	–0.23	0.39	–0.21	–0.38	2.34	–0.55	–0.46	–0.07	–0.09	–0.23	–0.13	0.42	0.29	1.97	–0.07	–0.07	0.01
	2001–07	0.19	11.36	0.27	1.29		0.45	0.96	0.72	1.23	1.49	1.39	2.91	1.34	1.80	0.23	0.13	0.17	0.59	0.47	1.29	2.05	1.01	0.27	0.92
BR	1995–2001	0.25	—	–0.15	—	–1.00		32.42	0.14	–0.97	–0.20	0.32	—	11.81	—	—	10.08	–0.25	—	—	–0.99	—	0.78	–0.87	0.53
	2001–07	0.48	0.63	–0.13	1.27	0.21		49.21	17.97	–0.15	–0.23	–0.69	—	3.62	5.70	—	0.01	–0.12	—	0.28	–1.00	10.33	1.12	1.00	1.19
ID	1995–2001	0.05	0.25	–0.19	0.29	0.21	–0.46		0.76	0.48	0.97	0.59	–0.03	0.94	0.10	0.23	0.20	0.04	–0.16	1.21	0.77	3.44	0.17	0.05	0.16
	2001–07	0.82	3.40	0.31	1.01	0.19	1.01		1.87	1.28	0.96	1.87	3.21	0.84	1.50	1.46	0.50	0.41	0.59	0.57	0.99	4.44	0.98	0.65	1.03
ML	1995–2001	0.28	1.02	0.03	0.47	0.43	–0.06	0.61		0.98	–0.00	0.17	0.76	0.83	0.63	–0.24	0.16	–0.09	0.13	0.93	—	0.29	0.21	0.14	0.19
	2001–07	0.37	3.05	1.01	1.26	0.47	0.48	2.31		0.98	0.73	1.60	3.92	1.90	1.54	2.43	0.54	0.75	0.04	0.81	3.55	3.83	0.92	0.77	1.00
PH	1995–2001	0.85	2.79	0.92	1.36	2.75	0.30	0.05	2.54		1.32	0.70	–0.50	0.59	–0.14	–0.38	0.42	0.44	–0.64	3.52	1.48	—	0.83	1.02	0.84
	2001–07	0.44	6.21	2.67	0.71	–0.12	0.51	2.94	1.25		0.36	0.03	5.98	1.35	5.03	9.59	–0.03	–0.08	1.21	–0.01	–0.13	0.89	0.59	0.35	0.56
SG	1995–2001	0.01	0.93	0.07	0.44	0.30	–0.72	—	–0.07	0.60		–0.22	0.17	0.22	0.05	0.12	–0.13	–0.30	–0.60	2.93	–0.33	–0.85	0.04	0.03	0.03
	2001–07	0.54	4.43	1.90	1.27	0.46	0.70	9.41	0.83	0.99		1.34	2.10	2.55	2.88	0.62	0.40	3.95	1.52	0.48	0.77	2.76	1.43	0.83	1.46
TH	1995–2001	0.05	0.74	0.12	0.53	0.41	–0.42	0.68	0.75	1.78	–0.34		0.70	0.74	0.96	–0.27	0.31	0.28	0.36	7.03	–0.36	—	0.19	0.23	0.15
	2001–07	0.94	4.58	1.80	1.59	0.86	1.62	2.75	2.08	1.70	0.94		4.14	3.53	2.61	3.25	0.56	0.86	4.32	1.15	8.22	6.63	1.42	0.99	1.51
VN	1995–2001	0.61	3.69	1.01	—	0.73	—	2.15	1.96	8.45	1.56	7.28		3.89	1.31	—	4.58	0.92	—	—	–0.85	4.56	1.86	1.19	1.63
	2001–07	1.43	1.57	0.84	2.06	1.45	—	3.36	3.61	1.62	1.14	2.19		2.65	2.63	3.37	8.49	4.02	4.05	7.19	8.85	1.36	2.53	1.83	2.23
AU	1995–2001	0.01	0.70	0.03	0.10	0.15	–0.49	–0.04	–0.18	–0.08	–0.02	–0.07	0.69		–0.03	–0.21	0.83	0.06	–0.32	2.66	1.25	–0.12	0.12	0.30	0.20
	2001–07	1.19	4.12	0.09	1.29	0.80	0.08	0.98	0.97	0.36	0.23	2.13	3.65		1.15	1.60	0.37	0.60	1.37	1.65	1.23	4.81	1.22	1.08	1.24
NZ	1995–2001	–0.23	0.63	–0.21	–0.14	–0.25	–0.88	0.16	0.02	0.73	–0.13	–0.06	3.00	–0.07		–0.18	0.50	0.18	–0.64	2.08	–0.40	–0.88	0.01	0.06	–0.00
	2001–07	0.44	1.55	0.31	0.62	0.90	0.68	1.49	0.64	1.08	2.04	1.42	0.72	1.29		1.16	0.52	0.50	0.89	0.97	–0.30	7.39	0.88	0.85	0.97
PNG	1995–2001	–0.60	0.55	–0.85	–0.62	0.40	—	0.83	–0.66	–0.27	–0.24	2.02	0.26	–0.26	–0.23		–0.20	4.09	—	—	—	—	–0.35	–0.54	–0.40
	2001–07	1.77	2.83	1.64	0.59	–0.07	—	0.16	3.22	0.80	0.15	0.27	15.42	2.33	0.70		1.76	–0.39	—	11.53	—	15.80	1.87	1.39	1.91
USA	1995–2001	–0.11	0.63	–0.01	–0.13	–0.06	–0.45	–0.26	0.06	0.45	0.15	–0.06	0.82	0.01	0.25	–0.56		0.30	–0.14	1.19	–0.12	–0.11	0.25	0.28	0.25
	2001–07	0.09	2.40	0.43	0.56	0.45	0.34	0.68	0.25	0.01	0.49	0.41	3.13	0.76	0.33	1.97		0.52	1.67	0.34	1.63	1.71	0.51	0.50	0.59
CA	1995–2001	–0.37	0.20	–0.34	–0.33	–0.46	–0.76	–0.31	–0.44	0.00	–0.26	–0.25	0.58	–0.10	0.10	–0.49	0.49		–0.14	1.26	0.19	0.46	0.41	0.05	0.36
	2001–07	0.60	2.24	0.81	1.16	1.18	2.97	2.10	1.50	0.90	2.39	0.93	6.13	1.35	1.72	1.28	0.46		2.00	1.61	1.53	4.72	0.51	1.64	0.61
CH	1995–2001	–0.25	2.57	–0.44	–0.36	–0.49	—	–0.73	–0.64	–0.15	–0.69	–0.70	—	–0.31	–0.37	–0.92	0.34	1.79		5.30	0.10	—	0.08	0.04	0.10
	2001–07	2.27	8.69	1.06	5.66	3.85	—	4.66	1.31	4.64	3.63	5.42	24.23	5.78	1.70	0.13	1.62	3.48		1.85	1.15	12.18	3.05	2.35	2.73
MX	1995–2001	–0.33	6.62	—	2.29	2.91	—	–0.14	1.49	1.73	0.40	1.03	—	0.58	3.73	—	1.11	0.55	–0.24		–0.04	—	1.07	0.57	2.27
	2001–07	2.08	5.73	1.74	1.32	0.58	13.87	2.12	0.83	3.55	0.39	1.66	11.06	5.36	0.73	—	0.59	1.11	2.13		2.92	7.86	0.63	1.63	0.72
PE	1995–2001	–0.24	0.20	–0.57	–0.30	–0.57	—	0.57	–0.79	–0.51	2.96	2.06	3.33	2.25	0.98	—	0.77	0.02	0.84	0.33		0.68	0.25	0.09	0.23
	2001–07	4.74	6.14	2.32	6.98	3.60	—	–0.34	–0.74	–0.56	–0.47	–0.34	4.57	1.74	4.61	0.52	2.10	11.47	5.00	1.10		–0.58	3.52	1.60	3.03
RU	1995–2001	–0.23	0.17	–0.64	0.11	–0.43	—	–0.64	–0.55	–0.63	0.45	–0.82	–0.51	–0.65	2.26	—	–0.44	–0.61	–0.07	2.35	0.07		–0.22	–0.05	–0.16
	2001–07	2.05	2.80	1.18	6.33	2.38	—	7.70	0.70	1.59	0.30	3.72	1.95	3.64	–0.27	–0.86	1.47	5.67	0.09	2.04	4.32		2.36	3.66	3.09
APEC(21)	1995–2001	0.05	0.30	0.12	0.03	0.03	–0.56	0.02	–0.06	0.37	–0.07	–0.19	0.57	0.11	0.04	–0.21	0.37	0.28	–0.13	1.17	0.03	–0.07	0.21	0.18	0.22
	2001–07	0.66	2.61	1.47	1.43	0.88	0.68	2.28	0.98	0.68	0.97	1.30	3.15	1.54	1.26	1.63	0.64	0.63	2.30	0.55	1.94	6.16	1.03	1.19	1.17
EU(15)	1995–2001	–0.19	0.28	–0.07	–0.23	–0.16	—	–0.50	–0.29	0.34	–0.19	–0.41	—	–0.05	–0.30	—	0.59	0.21	0.04	1.05	–0.33	0.54	0.20	0.03	0.05
	2001–07	0.42	2.45	0.44	1.34	0.51	—	0.78	0.77	0.28	0.98	0.56	1.82	1.28	0.84	—	0.58	0.70	0.90	1.01	1.31	2.64	0.89	0.99	0.95
WORLD	1995–2001	–0.06	0.71	–0.09	–0.04	0.09	–0.66	–0.15	–0.06	0.41	–0.12	–0.21	0.43	0.05	–0.10	–0.21	0.41	0.32	–0.03	2.05	–0.23	–0.21	0.20	0.14	0.20
	2001–07	0.79	2.82	1.32	1.51	1.01	2.00	1.99	0.99	0.66	1.10	1.32	2.94	1.50	1.20	1.66	0.71	0.70	1.68	0.64	2.12	3.63	1.10	1.12	1.23

Appendix Table 4: Trade Intensity Matrix of APEC Economies: 1995, 2001, 2007

Source: Calculated from Appendix Table 1 according to Trade intensity index of exporter I to importer j: Iij = (Xij/Xi.)/(X.j/X..) where Xij, Xi., X.j and X.. denote i's exports to j, i's total export, j's total import, and total world trade, respectively. Iij takes values either above or below 1.

Trade Intensity matrix of APEC Economies: 1995, 2001, 2007

EXPORT FROM	IMPORT TO	Japan	China	Hong Kong	South Korea	Ch.Taipei	Brunei	Indonesia	Malaysia	The Philippines	Singapore	Thailand	Vietnam	Australia	New Zealand	PNG	USA	Canada	Chile	Mexico	Peru	Russia	APEC(21)	EU(15)
JP	1995		1.947	1.652	2.654	3.564	0.427	2.812	2.476	2.871	2.118	3.192	0.895	1.617	1.335	1.099	1.814	0.407	0.660	0.912	0.447	0.220	1.595	0.401
	2001		2.120	2.015	2.938	3.607	0.709	2.800	2.282	3.115	2.032	3.203	1.599	1.935	1.425	0.715	1.685	0.458	0.460	0.452	0.711	0.225	1.588	0.425
	2007		2.474	1.831	3.167	4.190	0.663	1.670	1.977	2.731	1.808	3.746	1.636	1.805	1.724	1.103	1.470	0.545	0.733	0.872	0.571	0.922	1.678	0.379
CN	1995	2.892		6.374	1.689	1.133	0.330	1.208	0.562	1.240	0.959	0.845	2.088	0.966	0.567	0.433	1.095	0.319	0.881	0.148	0.648	0.937	1.643	0.327
	2001	3.272		6.093	2.204	1.128	0.332	1.883	1.010	0.933	1.210	1.021	2.457	1.361	0.794	0.442	1.142	0.354	1.213	0.301	0.689	1.291	1.554	0.409
	2007	2.028		5.086	1.919	1.286	0.355	1.362	1.364	1.268	1.441	1.028	2.008	1.339	0.876	0.902	1.396	0.587	1.198	0.584	1.023	1.430	1.445	0.509
HK	1995	0.922	13.097		0.606	1.449	0.200	0.764	0.582	2.072	1.161	0.667	1.577	1.218	0.687	0.695	1.435	0.469	1.133	0.255	0.011	0.151	1.624	0.377
	2001	1.140	10.172		0.840	1.458	1.382	0.777	0.714	1.544	1.121	1.080	1.030	1.199	0.702	0.285	1.241	0.432	0.855	0.270	0.291	0.141	1.676	0.384
	2007	1.062	7.800		0.865	1.361	0.326	0.683	0.872	1.687	1.102	1.137	1.439	1.152	0.736	0.143	0.988	0.364	0.378	0.278	0.248	0.157	1.802	0.357
SK	1995	2.066	2.891	2.243		1.694	—	2.960	1.544	2.141	2.185	1.393	4.662	1.110	—	—	1.273	0.444	1.625	0.853	—	0.937	1.522	0.309
	2001	2.123	3.341	2.195		2.330	0.563	3.844	1.460	2.585	1.510	1.337	4.178	1.467	0.880	0.380	1.163	0.381	1.509	0.637	1.295	0.791	1.499	0.348
	2007	1.717	3.568	1.688		2.339	0.275	2.044	1.441	2.449	1.903	1.263	3.186	1.144	0.929	0.256	0.900	0.349	2.771	1.223	0.932	1.332	1.538	0.328
Ch.Taipei	1995	1.786	4.794	3.629	0.793		0.286	1.927	2.128	2.271	1.720	2.023	1.826	2.182	1.083	0.265	1.638	0.520	0.531	0.668	0.370	0.060	1.784	0.408
	2001	2.010	1.067	7.666	1.249		0.481	2.116	2.082	2.683	1.836	1.882	5.099	1.126	0.772	0.372	1.262	0.358	0.571	0.370	0.742	0.271	1.645	0.399
	2007	1.560	4.025	4.897	1.326		0.270	1.617	2.099	4.190	2.533	2.255	5.883	1.229	1.142	0.201	0.966	0.286	0.395	0.386	0.635	0.208	1.829	0.278
BR	1995	8.750	—	0.015	—	1.189		0.059	0.124	0.595	3.928	8.950	—	0.671	—	—	0.113	0.044	0.000	—	0.940	—	1.825	0.224
	2001	9.142	1.140	0.011	5.366	0.002		1.823	0.117	0.009	2.810	11.714	0.001	6.437	3.001	—	0.692	0.019	0.000	0.004	0.005	0.000	2.118	0.020
	2007	7.721	0.497	0.004	4.951	0.002		31.194	1.143	0.005	1.055	1.601	—	12.122	9.320	—	0.418	0.010	0.000	0.003	0.000	0.000	2.180	0.020
ID	1995	3.836	1.423	0.867	2.258	2.030	1.188		1.355	2.025	2.285	0.989	2.932	1.728	0.987	1.902	0.877	0.239	0.662	0.242	0.163	0.024	1.584	0.381
	2001	4.471	1.080	0.801	3.138	2.333	1.977		2.639	2.219	5.302	2.055	2.075	3.327	1.251	3.096	0.772	0.195	0.599	0.182	0.391	0.140	1.606	0.367
	2007	5.011	1.371	0.497	2.768	1.518	1.458		4.191	3.343	5.445	2.797	2.441	2.695	1.567	3.164	0.744	0.178	0.392	0.192	0.274	0.181	1.668	0.313
ML	1995	1.878	1.003	1.402	1.023	1.678	5.642	1.637		1.576	8.241	2.779	1.563	1.340	0.894	2.011	1.362	0.252	0.306	0.512	—	0.114	1.645	0.357
	2001	2.583	1.197	1.609	1.574	2.222	15.939	3.125		2.239	9.413	4.144	1.950	2.363	1.637	1.967	1.132	0.175	0.361	0.327	0.148	0.188	1.679	0.362
	2007	2.209	1.418	1.554	1.584	1.814	8.760	3.861		2.976	8.652	5.177	2.717	3.053	2.114	2.837	1.140	0.200	0.156	0.404	0.241	0.219	1.715	0.336
PH	1995	2.367	0.470	1.237	0.949	1.768	0.248	0.900	1.172		2.316	3.275	3.048	0.718	0.457	0.690	2.340	0.347	0.620	0.233	0.151	—	1.682	0.441
	2001	3.044	0.681	1.717	1.522	3.974	0.623	0.727	2.889		3.996	4.596	0.705	0.711	0.286	0.356	1.543	0.247	0.149	0.226	0.320	0.054	1.679	0.514
	2007	3.509	1.838	3.881	1.477	2.480	0.447	1.367	4.674		3.680	2.916	1.781	0.952	1.120	2.024	1.241	0.190	0.176	0.194	0.127	0.031	1.813	0.466
SG	1995	1.178	0.918	2.256	1.031	2.217	17.918	—	12.516	2.921		4.139	6.512	1.938	1.181	5.852	1.202	0.150	0.235	0.179	0.117	0.642	1.648	0.338
	2001	1.484	1.209	3.105	1.804	3.090	17.332	4.104	14.492	3.885		4.734	6.273	2.631	1.608	9.768	0.863	0.093	0.114	0.270	0.120	0.139	1.667	0.356
	2007	1.163	1.562	3.520	1.476	2.039	8.923	12.950	12.102	4.214		4.324	4.471	3.387	2.569	5.407	0.639	0.245	0.097	0.221	0.062	0.102	1.751	0.279
TH	1995	2.537	1.144	1.363	0.533	1.307	1.638	1.795	1.797	1.314	5.718		3.566	1.217	0.599	1.496	1.176	0.336	0.266	0.106	0.246	0.000	1.478	0.381
	2001	2.964	1.213	1.768	0.885	1.765	2.957	3.695	3.492	2.723	4.514		4.438	2.120	1.363	1.443	1.140	0.339	0.392	0.292	0.216	0.157	1.534	0.430
	2007	2.861	1.578	1.895	0.811	1.452	2.298	4.114	4.805	3.921	3.706		5.143	3.408	1.986	2.050	0.922	0.330	0.692	0.340	0.567	0.230	1.571	0.359
VN	1995	4.121	2.075	0.727	—	2.342	—	1.834	1.301	1.221	2.908	0.489		3.292	0.509	—	0.220	0.303	—	—	1.270	0.510	1.291	0.606
	2001	3.232	2.606	0.738	1.266	1.703	0.343	3.101	1.875	3.760	3.867	2.337		7.039	0.599	1.378	0.398	0.201	0.244	0.131	0.115	1.641	1.406	0.533
	2007	3.034	1.214	0.403	1.066	1.431	—	3.124	3.005	4.090	2.722	2.216		7.094	0.682	1.567	1.521	0.410	0.318	0.451	0.252	0.577	1.632	0.492
AU	1995	3.496	1.712	1.045	3.191	2.505	1.289	4.120	2.025	2.513	2.191	1.729	1.241		26.465	51.393	0.420	0.519	0.636	0.122	0.176	0.172	1.656	0.281
	2001	3.748	1.706	1.195	3.649	2.638	1.944	4.630	1.768	1.654	2.437	2.036	1.478		28.512	51.879	0.545	0.417	0.444	0.147	0.516	0.191	1.541	0.321
	2007	4.584	2.288	0.561	3.329	2.352	0.698	3.053	1.753	1.351	1.430	2.738	1.738		27.819	50.684	0.436	0.392	0.392	0.238	0.369	0.240	1.624	0.314
NZ	1995	2.449	0.993	0.802	1.934	1.579	1.157	1.810	1.364	1.787	0.570	0.961	1.221	17.929		14.645	0.653	0.505	1.370	0.601	2.837	0.685	1.532	0.356
	2001	2.421	1.138	0.841	2.067	1.306	0.494	2.968	1.783	2.651	0.680	1.371	4.125	19.211		18.274	0.833	0.544	0.606	0.730	2.688	0.127	1.557	0.399
	2007	2.221	0.864	0.537	1.510	1.406	0.314	2.808	1.674	3.769	1.117	1.620	2.045	19.925		16.862	0.841	0.544	0.485	1.000	0.688	0.262	1.579	0.394
PNG	1995	3.797	1.056	0.389	2.900	0.165	—	0.284	0.593	5.422	0.401	0.570	0.163	29.000	6.467		0.122	0.012	—	—	—	—	1.701	0.484
	2001	3.245	1.903	0.126	2.274	0.420	—	1.212	0.426	5.638	0.688	4.311	0.286	40.929	11.072		0.138	0.090	—	0.000	—	0.016	1.816	0.392
	2007	3.857	1.463	0.110	1.104	0.148	—	0.361	0.693	4.666	0.289	1.798	0.911	41.689	6.549		0.170	0.024	—	0.001	0.000	0.044	1.903	0.339
USA	1995	1.662	0.790	0.641	1.633	1.798	0.470	0.726	0.985	1.622	1.068	0.785	0.186	1.632	1.053	0.351		6.676	1.972	8.959	2.005	0.437	1.343	0.534
	2001	1.525	0.727	0.672	1.425	1.493	0.734	0.610	1.072	1.611	1.348	0.894	0.229	1.522	1.409	0.187		6.311	1.695	6.194	2.226	0.472	1.347	0.580
	2007	1.305	0.907	0.582	1.241	1.509	0.461	0.479	0.943	1.365	1.338	0.760	0.336	1.497	1.195	0.293		7.911	2.364	7.110	2.631	0.388	1.358	0.574
CA	1995	0.671	0.469	0.167	0.380	0.347	0.023	0.285	0.135	0.209	0.073	0.143	0.054	0.357	0.240	0.063	5.240		0.458	0.463	0.354	0.055	1.911	0.148
	2001	0.399	0.291	0.107	0.234	0.152	0.014	0.204	0.071	0.132	0.054	0.119	0.053	0.271	0.260	0.036	4.882		0.362	0.304	0.487	0.091	1.984	0.121
	2007	0.494	0.342	0.116	0.279	0.228	0.026	0.293	0.124	0.209	0.121	0.137	0.132	0.353	0.446	0.043	5.766		0.561	0.669	0.548	0.156	1.981	0.209
CH	1995	2.742	0.707	0.143	2.104	2.391	—	1.232	0.359	0.738	0.201	0.672	—	0.331	0.341	0.753	0.986	0.186		0.932	18.057	—	1.140	0.701
	2001	2.381	1.610	0.097	1.538	1.229	—	0.420	0.150	0.486	0.077	0.282	0.088	0.237	0.261	0.085	1.024	0.429		2.105	28.277	0.124	1.121	0.697
	2007	2.608	2.446	0.051	2.437	1.774	—	0.474	0.104	0.985	0.102	0.465	0.336	0.384	0.192	0.022	0.935	0.675		2.186	11.666	0.212	1.290	0.657
MX	1995	0.290	0.030	—	0.069	0.050	—	0.041	0.036	0.022	0.146	0.046	—	0.102	0.030	—	9.042	1.266	3.228		2.442	—	3.107	0.177
	2001	0.076	0.049	0.026	0.087	0.065	0.001	0.015	0.035	0.016	0.085	0.043	0.007	0.057	0.058	—	4.966	0.545	0.937		1.131	0.014	1.966	0.090
	2007	0.170	0.113	0.041	0.104	0.067	0.007	0.021	0.042	0.056	0.073	0.064	0.030	0.187	0.059	0.088	5.996	0.882	1.422		1.847	0.036	1.986	0.145
PE	1995	1.359	2.504	0.236	1.072	1.955	—	0.560	0.820	1.350	0.015	0.296	0.154	0.174	0.065	—	1.130	0.778	8.757	1.948		0.284	1.073	0.752
	2001	1.075	1.719	0.108	0.757	0.753	—	1.009	0.180	0.458	0.064	1.117	0.459	0.530	0.141	0.097	1.388	0.588	16.320	0.833		0.592	1.092	0.703
	2007	1.915	1.782	0.086	1.332	0.955	—	0.124	0.013	0.067	0.009	0.176	0.360	0.321	0.199	0.031	1.390	2.390	20.283	0.592		0.030	1.301	0.476
RU	1995	0.592	1.638	0.101	0.346	0.311	—	0.125	0.461	0.274	0.246	0.347	1.708	0.032	0.009	—	0.414	0.046	0.087	0.039	0.261		0.405	0.811
	2001	0.687	1.597	0.058	0.566	0.230	—	0.074	0.316	0.102	0.577	0.110	0.833	0.015	0.046	0.016	0.234	0.019	0.119	0.061	0.519		0.372	0.963
	2007	0.640	0.869	0.029	0.902	0.211	—	0.118	0.147	0.086	0.195	0.122	0.340	0.015	0.008	0.000	0.185	0.041	0.026	0.062	0.484		0.325	1.155
APEC(21)	1995	1.372	2.246	1.459	1.409	1.787	1.442	1.359	1.796	1.804	1.573	1.515	1.462	1.436	1.418	2.090	1.501	1.936	1.073	2.620	0.903	0.327	1.557	0.407
	2001	1.511	1.686	1.787	1.485	1.665	1.867	1.609	1.774	1.737	1.637	1.532	1.589	1.503	1.625	2.083	1.440	1.858	0.959	1.840	1.207	0.382	1.555	0.417
	2007	1.448	1.641	1.957	1.480	1.607	1.077	1.816	1.819	1.802	1.583	1.559	1.723	1.568	1.715	2.127	1.418	1.833	1.217	1.790	1.172	0.608	1.544	0.442
EU(15)	1995	0.314	0.356	0.232	0.289	0.318	0.475	0.425	0.328	0.231	0.288	0.342	—	0.549	0.459	0.116	0.383	0.216	0.428	0.324	0.376	0.638	0.340	1.487
	2001	0.312	0.305	0.273	0.264	0.281	—	0.285	0.286	0.252	0.304	0.293	0.243	0.571	0.408	—	0.496	0.227	0.529	0.249	0.378	1.423	0.389	1.545
	2007	0.285	0.316	0.194	0.281	0.243	1.432	0.195	0.292	0.223	0.329	0.225	0.199	0.598	0.392	0.090	0.525	0.260	0.431	0.350	0.321	1.282	0.401	1.660

Appendix Table 5: Consolidated Trade Intensity Matrix: 1995, 2001, 2007

Source: Calculated from Appendix Table 2 using the same formula as in Appendix Table 4.

Appendix Table 5
Consolidated Trade Intensity Matrix: 1995, 2001, 2007

EXPORT FROM	IMPORT TO	Japan	China	East Asia 3	ASEAN 7	Oceania 3	USA	America 4	Russia	APEC(21)	EU(15)
Japan	1995	—	1.95	2.27	2.49	1.55	1.81	0.52	0.22	1.60	0.40
	2001	—	2.12	2.25	2.47	1.83	1.68	0.46	0.22	1.59	0.43
	2007	—	2.47	1.26	2.22	1.78	1.47	0.67	0.92	1.68	0.38
China	1995	2.89	—	3.71	0.93	0.88	1.10	0.34	0.94	1.64	0.33
	2001	3.27	—	3.61	1.23	1.25	1.14	0.38	1.29	1.55	0.41
	2007	2.03	—	3.15	1.37	1.26	1.40	0.64	1.43	1.44	0.51
East Asia 3	1995	1.5	2.1	2.5	2.6	1.6	1.9	0.6	0.2	1.7	0.4
	2001	1.7	1.8	2.4	2.1	1.6	1.5	0.4	0.2	1.4	0.4
	2007	1.4	1.8	2.1	1.7	1.3	1.1	0.5	0.7	1.3	0.3
ASEAN 7	1995	2.14	1.04	1.50	3.29	1.49	1.22	0.24	0.27	1.60	0.37
	2001	2.70	1.20	2.05	4.12	2.44	1.00	0.22	0.20	1.63	0.39
	2007	2.51	1.50	1.89	4.44	3.18	0.89	0.26	0.18	1.70	0.33
Oceania 3	1995	3.30	1.54	1.88	1.98	8.35	0.45	0.47	0.27	1.63	0.30
	2001	3.51	1.61	2.14	2.19	7.97	0.59	0.37	0.18	1.55	0.34
	2007	4.20	2.04	1.75	1.92	7.66	0.49	0.39	0.24	1.62	0.33
USA	1995	1.66	0.79	1.22	0.96	1.50	—	6.64	0.44	1.34	0.53
	2001	1.53	0.73	1.12	1.11	1.49	—	6.01	0.47	1.35	0.58
	2007	1.30	0.91	1.01	0.95	1.43	—	7.14	0.39	1.36	0.57
America 4	1995	0.74	0.45	0.30	0.15	0.28	5.60	0.41	0.05	1.98	0.20
	2001	0.37	0.28	0.15	0.09	0.19	4.71	0.29	0.07	1.93	0.14
	2007	0.61	0.49	0.26	0.13	0.29	5.29	0.59	0.11	1.90	0.23
Russia	1995	0.59	1.64	0.23	0.35	0.03	0.41	0.05	—	0.40	0.81
	2001	0.69	1.60	0.26	0.34	0.02	0.23	0.05	—	0.37	0.96
	2007	0.64	0.87	0.37	0.16	0.01	0.18	0.06	—	0.32	1.15
APEC(21)	1995	1.37	2.25	1.52	1.60	1.44	1.50	1.97	0.33	1.56	0.41
	2001	1.51	1.69	1.66	1.66	1.53	1.44	1.80	0.38	1.56	0.42
	2007	1.45	1.64	1.71	1.69	1.60	1.42	1.76	0.61	1.54	0.44
EU(15)	1995	0.31	0.36	0.27	0.31	0.52	0.38	0.26	0.64	0.34	1.49
	2001	0.31	0.31	0.27	0.29	0.54	0.50	0.25	1.42	0.39	1.54
	2007	0.29	0.32	0.23	0.27	0.56	0.52	0.30	1.28	0.40	1.66

Appendix Table 6: Ratios of Commodity, Services Trade, and Direct Investment to GDP: 1995 and 2007

Sources: Calculated by the author based on the values (in U.S. dollars) at current prices from the following four sets of statistics, April 2010:
GDP: UN Statistical Division, National Accounts Main Aggregate Database, supplemented by Chinese Taipei's country statistics.
Commodity exports and imports: Appendix Table 1 above, at current price.
Services exports and imports: World Bank, *World Development Indicators*, online database.
Direct investment (outward and inward): UNCTAD, *Foreign Direct Investment Statistics*, online database.

Appendix Table 6

Ratios of Commodity, Services Trade, and Direct Investment to GDP (%)

	Commdity export		Commodity import		Service export		Service import		Outward investment		Inward investment	
	1995	2007	1995	2007	1995	2007	1995	2007	1995	2007	1995	2007
Japan	8.44	16.30	6.40	12.87	1.08	2.90	3.72	3.39	0.43	1.68	0.00	0.51
South Korea	23.20	35.41	25.07	31.21	3.01	5.86	3.38	7.86	0.66	1.46	0.24	0.25
China	19.66	35.20	17.06	24.37	2.17	3.57	2.09	3.74	0.26	0.65	4.96	2.41
Hong Kong	120.41	168.78	133.58	195.78	21.55	40.35	12.89	19.89	17.33	25.67	4.31	28.91
Chi Taipei	44.16	61.86	33.92	53.89	4.77	8.17	7.46	9.04	1.09	2.93	0.57	2.15
Brunei	44.54	57.62	74.22	28.94				0.00	0.91	0.31	12.32	1.50
Indonesia	21.91	26.36	18.30	23.94	2.12	2.79	5.00	5.57	0.59	1.11	1.99	1.60
Malaysia	80.26	94.43	84.29	77.83	9.97	15.10	12.90	14.89	2.70	5.89	6.30	4.50
Philippines	23.61	34.89	38.23	45.99	9.04	6.80	6.21	5.14	0.13	2.39	1.97	2.03
Singapore	140.91	179.34	148.34	138.07	27.28	41.75	16.44	43.55	8.09	7.37	13.74	14.46
Thailand	33.61	66.29	42.13	53.04	6.78	12.23	9.05	15.53	0.53	0.71	1.23	3.89
Vietnam	27.60	68.38	56.92	93.45	6.27	8.45	6.27	9.72	0.00	0.21	8.58	9.49
Australia	13.72	14.92	14.95	15.89	3.67	4.19	3.96	4.07	0.85	2.56	3.12	2.35
New Zealand	22.41	20.67	22.77	21.18	5.87	7.05	6.36	6.90	2.91	2.18	4.65	2.12
PNG	54.63	75.16	26.07	42.60	4.13	4.84	12.40	29.04		0.13	12.29	1.55
Canada	32.55	44.40	27.76	38.96	3.93	6.71	5.44	8.63	1.94	5.68	1.57	11.47
Chile	22.26	40.14	22.08	25.17	3.89	5.37	4.02	5.92	1.04	2.34	4.10	8.82
Mexico	15.44	26.68	14.31	22.03	3.22	1.73	3.95	2.28		0.81	3.04	2.42
Peru	10.39	25.70	14.32	17.11	1.86	2.98	2.80	3.82	0.01	0.75	4.76	4.98
USA	7.96	8.46	10.50	13.58	2.47	3.44	1.65	2.49	1.25	2.28	0.80	1.69
Russia	20.32	21.61	15.27	17.22	2.10	3.02	3.86	4.46	0.15	3.53	0.52	0.41
APEC21	13.84	21.13	14.13	20.67	2.58	4.75	3.15	4.55	1.05	2.55	1.04	2.51
EU15	26.69	30.53	22.84	30.94					1.24	5.68	0.84	3.66

References

ABAC. *APEC Means Business: Building Prosperity for our Community*. Singapore, 1996.

———. *Facing Globalization the APEC Way: Report to the APEC Leaders*. Brunei Darussalum, 2000.

ABAC and PECC. *An APEC Trade Agenda? The Political Economy of a Free Trade Area of the Asia Pacific: A Joint Study*. August 2006.

APEC. *A Mid-term Stocktake of Progress Towards the Bogor Goals — Busan Roadmap to Bogor Goals*. Submitted to 17th APEC Ministerial Meeting by SOM Chair. Busan, Korea, 15–16 November 2005*a*.

———. *Bogor Goals Mid-term Stocktake — Project Team Experts' Report*, with attachment: Progress on Specific Trade and Investment Barriers. 2005*b*.

———. "Ha Noi Action Plan: To Implement the Busan Roadmap towards the Bogor Goals". 18–19 November 2006 <http://www.apec.org>.

———. *The APEC Initiative for Strengthening Regional Economic Integration*. September 2007.

———. *Progress Report on the APEC Regional Economic Integration Agenda*. Submitted to APEC Ministerial Meeting Retreat Session by SOM Chair, 2008.

———. *Stocktake of Structural Reform Activities in APEC*. 2009.

APEC/EC. APEC Economic Committee. *The State of Economic and Technical Cooperation in APEC*. November 1996.

APEC/EPG. APEC/Eminent Persons Group. *A Vision for APEC: Towards an Asia Pacific Economic Community*. Singapore, October 1993.

———. *Achieving the APEC Vision: Free and Open Trade in the Asia Pacific*. Singapore, August 1994.

———. *Implementing the APEC Vision*. Singapore, August 1995.

APEC/FM. The Second APEC Finance Ministers Meeting. "Joint Ministerial Statement". Bali, Indonesia, April 1995.

———. 16th APEC Finance Ministers Meeting. "Joint Ministerial Statement 2009".

APEC/LM. "APEC Economic Leaders' Declaration of Common Resolve". Bogor, Indonesia, 1994.

———. "APEC Economic Leaders' Declaration for Action". Osaka, November 1995.

———. "APEC Economic Leaders' Declaration, Connecting the APEC Community". Vancouver, Canada, November 1997.

———. "Leaders' Agenda to Implement Structural Reform (LAISR)". Santiago, Chile, November 2004.

———. Lima "APEC Leaders' Statement on the Global Economy". 22 November 2008.

———. "Leaders' Declaration: Sustaining Growth, Connecting the Region". The 17th APEC Economic Leaders' Meeting. Singapore, 14–15 November 2009.

APEC/MM. *The Osaka Action Agenda: Implementation of the Bogor Declaration*, Part I Liberalization and Facilitation; Part II Economic and Technical Cooperation. November 1995.

———. *APEC, MAPA 1996, Manila Action Plan for APEC*; Vol. II Individual Action Plans; Vol. III Collective Action Plans; Vol. IV Progress Report on APEC Ecotech Joint Activities and Framework Declaration on Ecotech 1996.

———. "Joint Statement by Ministers". Vancouver, November 1997.

———. "Joint Statement by Ministers". Bandar Seri Begawan, Brunei Darussalam, November 2000.

———. "Joint Ministerial Statement on Structural Reform". August 2008.

APEC/Policy Support Unit (PSU). *Progressing towards the APEC Bogor Goals Perspectives of the APEC Policy Support Unit*. January 2010.

APEC/TM. *APEC Meeting of Ministers Responsible for Trade: Statement of the Chair*. Kuching, Malaysia, June 1998.

APEC SOM. *APEC Model Measures for RTAs/FTAs*. 18 November 2008.

ASEAN. *Towards an East Asian Community: Region of Peace, Prosperity and Progress*. East Asian Vision Group Report, 2001.

———. "Chairman's Statement of the 12th ASEAN Plus Three Summit". Cha-am Hua Hin, Thailand, 24 October 2008.

———. "Chairman's Statement of the 4th East Asian Summit". Cha-am Hua Hin, Thailand, 24 October 2008.

Asian Development Bank. "Inclusive Growth toward a Harmonious Society". Asian Development Review, 25th anniversary edition, 25, no. 1, 2 (Jun–Dec 2008).

China-Japan-ROK Trilateral Summit. "Joint Statement for Tripartite Partnership". Fukuoka, Japan, 13 December 2008*a*.

———. *Action Plan for Promoting Trilateral Cooperation among the People's Republic of China, Japan and the Republic of Korea*. Fukuoka, 13 December 2008*b*.

———. *Action Agenda for Improvement of the Business Environment*. December 2008*c*.

———. *Joint Report and Policy Proposals on the Possible Roadmap toward China-Japan-ROK FTA* [in Japanese]. Jointly by DRC China, NIRA Japan and KIEP ROK. December 2008.

———. "Joint Statement on the Tenth Anniversary of trilateral Cooperation among the People's Republic of China, Japan and the Republic of Korea". Beijing, China, 10 October 2009.

Drysdale, P. and T. Terada, eds. *Asia Pacific Economic Cooperation? Critical Perspectives on the World Economy*, 5 volumes. Routledge, 2008.

East Asian Summit (EAS) Joint Expert Group for Feasibility. *Towards an East Asia FTA: Modality and Road Map, A Report*. July 2006.

Elek, Andrew. "The Mid-term Bogor Goals: Strategic Issues and Options". In *Asia Pacific Economic Cooperation*, edited by P. Drysdale and T. Terada. 2005.

Elms, Deborah. "Evolution of the Trans-Pacific Partnership (TPP) Talks". Presented at the PECC Conference on "A Post 2010 Trade Agenda for the Asia-Pacific", 6–7 July 2010.

Feinberg, R.E. and Ye Zhao, eds. *Assessing APEC's Progress: Trade, Ecotech & Institutions*. A Project of the APEC International Assessment Network (APIAN). Singapore: Institute of Southeast Asian Studies, 2001.

Group on Asia Pacific Economic Integration. *Economic Integration in the Asia Pacific Region and the Options for Japan*. Ministry of Foreign Affairs, Government of Japan, April 1993.

Hatoyama, Yukio. *Japan's New Commitment to Asia — Toward the Realization of an East Asian Community*. Singapore, 15 November 2009.

IAP Study Group. *APEC's Progress toward the Bogor Target: A Quantitative Assessment of Individual Action Plans*. PECC Japan Committee, Tokyo, 1997.

———. *APEC's Progress toward the Bogor Target: A Quantitative Assessment of 1997 IAP/CAP*. PECC Japan Committee, Tokyo, 1998.

IDE/JETRO and KIEP. "Toward Closer Japan-Korea Economic Relationships: Proposal for Formulating a 21st Century Relationship: Joint Communique". 23 May 2000.

IDE/JETRO. *Joint Study Report: ASEAN-Japan Comprehensive Economic Partnership. Visions and Tasks Ahead*. 2003.

Ishido, Hikaru. *Database on Service Trade Liberalization by APEC Economies*. Mimeographed. November 2009.

JICA. Japan International Cooperation Agency. *APEC Partners for Progress (PFP) Research Report*. Tokyo, 1995.

Kim Sangkyom, Innwon Park, and Soonchan Park. *Economic Impact of an FTAAP: Implications and Significance for Regional Economic Integration*. December 2009.

Koh Tommy, Lee Tsao Yuan, and Arun Mahizhnan. "Integrating the Business Community in the APEC Process: Genesis of the Pacific Basin Forum".

In *APEC at 20: Recall, Reflect, Remake*, edited by Kesavapany and Lim. Singapore: Institute of Southeast Asian Studies, 2009.

Obama, Barack. "Remarks on the U.S. Relationship with the Nations of Asia". At the Suntory Hall, Tokyo, 13 November 2009.

Pacific Basin Cooperation Study Group. *Report on the Pacific Basin Cooperation Concept*. 1978. Reprinted in *Asia Pacific Economic Cooperation*, edited by P. Drysdale and T. Terada.

PECC. Implementing the APEC Bogor Declaration: A PECC Statement to APEC. July 1995.

Rudd, Kevin. "It's Time to Build an Asia Pacific Community". Address to the Asia Society Australian Centre. Sydney, 4 June 2008.

Soesastro, Hadi. "An 'Agenda-driven' Reform for APEC". *APEC Perspectives 2006: Towards a Dynamic Community for Sustainable Development and Prosperity*. APEC Study Center, Monash University and APEC, November 2006.

———. "Revamping APEC's Conceted Unilateral Liberalization". In *APEC at 20: Recall, Reflect, Remake*, edited by K. Kesavapany and Hank Lim. Singapore: Institute of Southeast Asian Studies, 2009.

Tong, Kurt. Testimony of Kurt Tong, acting U.S. senior official for APEC. "The Future of APEC". House Foreign Affairs Subcommittee on Asia, the Pacific and the Global Environment, 14 October 2009.

"Trans-Pacific Strategic Economic Partnership: Agreement (TPP)". By Brunei Darussalam, Chile, New Zealand, and Singapore, 2004.

University of South California / Marshall School of Business. *Rules of Origin Regimes and their Impact on Business in the APEC Region — Rules of Origin: Facilitators or Frictions*. Commissioned by ABAC and submitted to APEC conference in Sydney, September 2007.

U.S. Office of USTR. *2010 Trade Policy Agenda and 2009 Annual Report*. 5 March 2010.

Woo, Yuen Pao. "A Review of the APEC Individual Action Plan Peer Review Process". In *The Future of APEC and Regionalism in Asia Pacific: Perspectives from the Second Trade*, edited by PECC. CSIS Indonesia and PECC, 2005.

World Bank. *What is Inclusive Growth?* Prepared by Elena Ianchovichina and Susanna Lundstrom, 2009.

Yamazawa, Ippei. "On Pacific Economic Integration". *Economic Journal* 102, no. 415 (1992): 1519–29. Reprinted in *Asia Pacific Economic Cooperation*, edited by Drysdale and Terada.

———. "APEC's New Development and Its Implications for Nonmember Developing Countries". *Developing Economies* 34, no. 2 (1996).

———. *APEC's Progress toward the Bogor Target: A Quantitative Assessment of 1997 IAP/CAP*. PECC Japan Committee, 1998.

———. "On Japan-Korea FTA". *The Developing Economies. 2000.*

———. "Asia Pacific Economic Cooperation (APEC): Challenges and Tasks for the

Twenty-first Century". Proceedings of the 25th Pacific Trade and Development Conference in Osaka, June 1999. London: Routledge, 2000.

———. "APEC FTA vs. East Asian Summit FTA: Free Trade Agreements in the Asia-Pacific". In *Driving Growth — APEC's Destiny: Priorities and Strategies for APEC's Future in the 21st Century*. Australian APEC Study Centre, 2008.

———. "APEC at 20: Assessment of Trade/Investment Liberalization, Facilitation and Ecotech Activities". In *APEC at 20: Recall, Reflect, Remake*, edited by K. Kesavapany and Hank Lim. Singapore: Institute of Southeast Asian Studies, 2009.

Yamazawa, Ippei and S. Urata. "APEC's Progress in Trade and Investment Liberalization and Facilitation". 1999. Reprinted in Yamazawa (2000) and in *Asia Pacific Economic Cooperation*, edited by Drysdale and Terada.

Index

W

About the Author

Ippei Yamazawa received his doctorate in economics from Hitotsubashi University, Tokyo, where he is now Professor Emeritus. He has served as President, International University of Japan (2003–6) and President, Institute of Developing Economies/JETRO (1998–2003). He has been a regular participant in the Pacific Trade and Development Conference (until 1999) and the Pacific Economic Cooperation Conference (until 2003). He was a member of the APEC Eminent Persons Group (1993–95), coordinator of the APEC Study Center Japan Consortium (1995–present), and consultant for the APEC IAP peer review process (on Australia, 2002–3). His books include *APEC: Challenges and Tasks in the Twenty-First Century* (ed.) (Routledge, 2000) and *Japan-ASEAN Comprehensive Economic Partnership: Vision and Agenda* (IDE/JETRO, 2003). He received the Foreign Minister's commendation for his long-time contribution to PECC and APEC.

www.ingramcontent.com/pod-product-compliance
Lightning Source LLC
Chambersburg PA
CBHW021830020426
42334CB00014B/568

* 9 7 8 9 8 1 4 3 1 1 6 3 2 *